Collage Lab

First published in the United States of America by
Quarry Books, a member of
Quayside Publishing Group
100 Cummings Center
Suite 406-L
Beverly, Massachusetts 01915-6101
Telephone: (978) 282-9590
Fax: (978) 283-2742
www.quarrybooks.com
Visit www.Craftside.Typepad.com for a behind-the-scenes peek at our crafty world!

Library of Congress Cataloging-in-Publication Data

Shay, Bee.
  Collage lab : experiments, investigations, and exploratory projects / Bee Shay.
       p. cm.
  Includes index.
  ISBN-13: 978-1-59253-565-1
  ISBN-10: 1-59253-565-8
  1. Collage. I. Title.
  TT910.S429 2010
  702.81'2—dc22
                                                      2009022988

ISBN-13: 978-1-59253-565-1
ISBN-10: 1-59253-565-8

10 9 8 7 6 5 4 3 2

Cover Design: bradhamdesign.com
Book Layout: Megan Jones Design
Artwork: Bee Shay, except where otherwise noted
Photography: lightstream

Printed in China

Collage Lab

BEVERLY MASSACHUSETTS

EXPERIMENTS, INVESTIGATIONS, AND EXPLORATORY PROJECTS

BEE SHAY

QUARRY BOOKS

Contents

UNIT 3

Gesso

UNIT 1

Building the Foundation

Color

UNIT 4

UNIT 5

Surface Design

UNIT 2

Texture

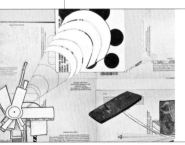

Line and Form

UNIT 6

Introduction

JOURNEYS BEGIN IN MANY WAYS. My initial experience with collage began in 1995 at the end of an artistic dry spell. As they say in sailing, I was "in irons." In short, I was going nowhere fast creatively and my quality of life was directly affected. A new attitude was needed to restore the spirit. As a teacher I felt that I had nothing new to offer my students, and that translated to not teaching, which in and of itself was detrimental to my work. My students have always infused me, given me energy and drive; without them, it was more difficult to surface.

Old habits die hard, and I found myself fighting those original skill sets that had been my vocation for so long in a struggle to learn new ways to express my artistic self. By giving the hands new things to play with, it didn't take long to understand that just getting my hands moving started the dialogue between them and my heart. It was up to me to get my head out of the way.

Soon I discovered that exploration and experimentation in my journals was the ticket. Before long the flood of creative work found me staying up through the wee hours of the morning in the quiet of my home, children nestled in their beds with no one to interrupt the flow. The desire to make things, anything, became insatiable. Every possible minute was spent playing, exploring, learning, succeeding, and not succeeding. Not liking to use the word *failure*, I draw on a quote from Thomas Edison when he was asked about his many attempts to invent the lightbulb. He remarked, "If I find ten thousand ways something won't work, I haven't failed. I am not discouraged,

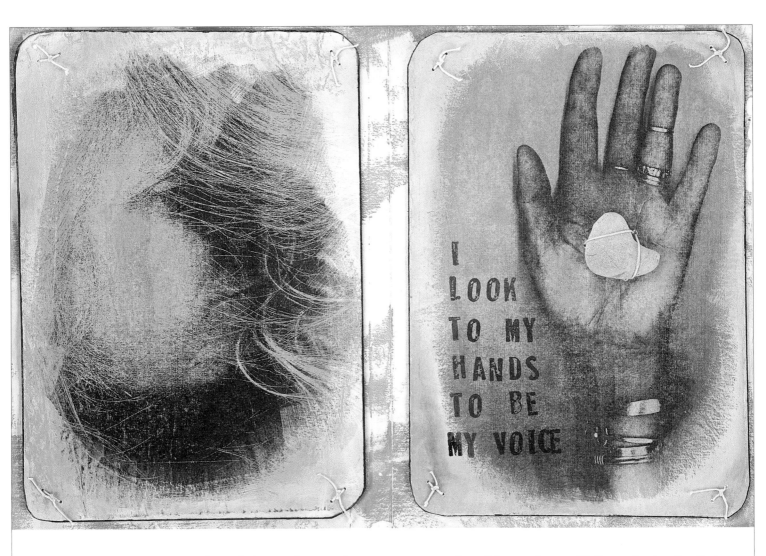

because every wrong attempt discarded is another step forward." These words couldn't be more applicable to the creative process.

This book is about getting your hands moving and getting your head out of the way. By following a set of simple steps that are not restrictive, without ties to any particular outcome, you will teach yourself what works best for you, and what doesn't work for you at all. Most importantly, you will come away from this experience with the understanding that it's not about the product, it's about the dance.

Now is the time to open the pages, gather your tools, and begin to explore, experiment, and enjoy the process of learning new. Go forward artfully.

Overview

COLLAGE LAB IS STRUCTURED to encourage the building of a visual vocabulary by working through the fifty-two labs comprising the twelve units. Each lab can be experienced on an independent basis. Once the basic vocabulary has been learned, the ability to create a well-executed, cohesive, and interesting collage will have been attained.

There are a few basics about using this book that will be helpful. First, each unit contains four or five labs that are all structured in the same format. You will find the following in each of the labs:

- Materials
- Instructions
- Play and Experiment
- Food for Thought

MATERIALS contains the supply list for completing the lab. **INSTRUCTIONS** are the basic steps for working through a process. **PLAY AND EXPERIMENT** shows options and variations to explore. Finally, **FOOD FOR THOUGHT** encourages evaluation of the work just completed. It is a time to make note of things of interest, what worked, what didn't, personal preferences and materials used, and which results they yielded. Write on the back of the work or on a separate page; make notes on anything that will enable you to remember down the road what was learned from working through these labs.

Seeing, doing, learning is the key to keeping the knowledge and information that has been acquired along the way through experience and will build a useful and very personal reference guide for years to come.

Consider keeping a journal of your labs. As work progresses through the labs, place it in the journal to create a personal reference volume. Include what works for you, what doesn't, notes about materials and methods, sources, and literal examples of the work to refer back to. When completed it will be as individual as the person creating it. The use of a commercially available blank journal is fine, or you can construct one to use for a more personal and unique reference book. When filing your labs, consider filing in the order that they are presented in the book. Although the labs are independent, they are laid out in a beginning-to-end fashion that makes chronological sense when viewed overall and might make it easier to refer back to in the future.

The labs are independent of one another and do not need to be worked in any specific order. Pick and choose what is appealing when time and inclination are available. Set aside a few hours of uninterrupted time to really focus. Adding new ideas and experimentation to the Play and Experiment portion is heartily encouraged.

Lastly, but definitely not least, enjoy the experience. Do not think of this as work; think of it as a creative challenge, an expedition. It is with experimentation and focus that new and innovative ideas spring. There are no mistakes, only results. There are no judgments, just personal preferences. No one is going to grade the work or critique it or even see it unless you willingly ask anyone to, so don't. This is for you and your eyes only and meant not to be great works of art or beautiful projects but rather the visual vocabulary that will

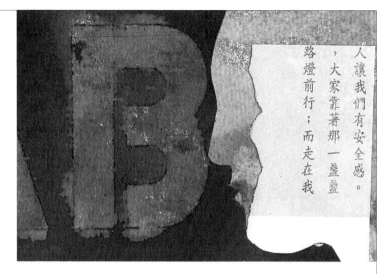

Artist: Fred B. Mullett

enable you to move forward and create work that is filled with texture, color, and meaning. Of course, you may very well end up with results that you are thrilled with, and those are the pieces you may choose to hang, frame, or share.

Good luck and enjoy the process. Let me hear from you about what is working and what is not. Remember always: it is not about the product, it's about the dance.

Building the Foundation

IT DOESN'T MAKE SENSE to ice the cake before it is baked or put the roof on a house until the sides are closed in. The same holds true for collage work. Achieving depth is one of the major keys to a successful collage. Even when the final product appears simplistic, building a rich and complex substrate on which the composition sits will allow the focal pieces to command attention. The resulting visual communication is basic and intriguing all at the same time. The dichotomy is what creates interest without hitting the viewer over the head.

This unit provides a quick overview and introduction to four basic surfaces on which to build your collage: gesso, paper, imagery, and washed substrates. They are by no means the only ways to start but are a good representation of the fundamentals and will aid in expanding your visual toolbox.

There is lots of room for exploration and experimentation, so feel free to follow any path of curiosity that gets sparked . . . that's what this is all about.

Artist: Lynne Perrella

Basic Gesso Surface

LEARNING OBJECTIVE: To become familiar with using gesso as a textural medium for creating interest on the collage substrate.

- watercolor paper (inexpensive 140 lb. cold press) for substrate

- gesso

- small jar of acrylic craft paint (light color)

- brush (at least 1" [2.5 cm]-wide)

- sponge (sea sponge and/or household sponge)

- plastic wrap

- graining comb (or lid from plastic container cut with pinking shears)

- corks, bottle caps, small scraps of wood, rubber stamps or anything three-dimensional that can make an impression or mark in the gesso

INSTRUCTIONS

STEP 1: Tint the gesso with craft paint to make it easier to see while you learn.

STEP 2: Lay a thick layer of gesso over the watercolor paper.

STEP 3: Wait a minute or two for the gesso to set up and get a little tacky.

STEP 4: Using the suggestions on page 13, create foundations of texture in various ways.

STEP 5: Allow to dry.

Play and Experiment

EXAMPLE 1: Lay down a layer of tinted gesso. When dry, lay down a second layer tinted a different color and pull a graining comb through the gesso to create textures and reveal substrate.

EXAMPLE 2: Pull a graining comb through gesso to create just textures.

EXAMPLE 3: Lay down a heavy layer of tinted gesso. On another substrate, lay down another layer of tinted gesso of a different color. Put both pieces of substrate together, then pull apart.

EXAMPLE 4: Sponge gesso onto substrate to create peaks and valleys.

EXAMPLE 5: Using masking tape, cover areas of the substrate, then apply layer of gesso and let dry. Remove tape.

EXAMPLE 6: Print with carved stamp, rubber stamp, or household object using gesso. Apply gesso to surface of carving, stamp, or object, using a sponge for best results.

EXAMPLE 7: Lay down a layer of sponged, tinted gesso. Using a different tinted gesso, sponge bold geometric shapes.

EXAMPLE 8: Lay down a layer of gesso and write in it with the wrong end of a paintbrush to reveal substrate.

EXAMPLE 9: Press, swirl, and scrape with miscellaneous household objects into gesso.

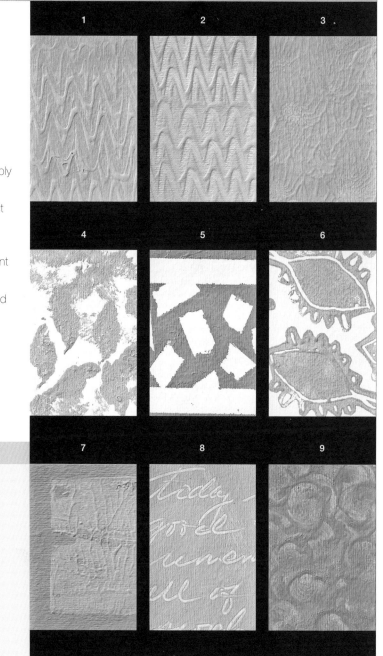

FOOD FOR THOUGHT

- How does the gesso change once dried?
- What happens when subsequent coats of gesso are applied to a dried texture surface?
- What worked best?
- What was difficult?
- List ten other common household objects that could make impressions.

Basic Paper Surface

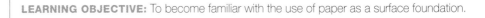

Materials

- watercolor paper (inexpensive 140 lb. cold press)
- matte medium (matte or glossy)
- brush (at least 1" [2.5 cm]-wide)
- text-weight paper
- tissue paper
- construction paper
- cardstock
- newspaper
- magazines or catalogs
- scrap paper of any sort

LEARNING OBJECTIVE: To become familiar with the use of paper as a surface foundation.

INSTRUCTIONS

STEP 1: Prepare papers, using the Play and Experiment suggestions.

STEP 2: Apply papers to watercolor paper, using matte medium as an adhesive.

STEP 3: When completed, final coat surface with matte medium.

STEP 4: Create at least ten pieces of foundation texture.

STEP 5: Allow to dry.

Play and Experiment

ROW 1: Tear long and short strips of paper the same width but different lengths to use together. Make grids or stripes or tear into small pieces and scatter.

ROW 2: Lay down a thick layer of matte medium and, while still damp, apply tissue paper and bunch it up to create wrinkles.

ROW 3: Cut or punch paper into shapes for application. Use both the positive and negative forms together and separately.

FOOD FOR THOUGHT

- Take note of how different papers take varied amounts of matte medium to stay flat.

- How does glossy paper differ from matte paper in resulting texture?

- Is thicker paper more difficult to work with than thinner paper such as tissue?

- Which papers are you most comfortable with?

- Which papers were most difficult to work with?

- Which papers surprised you with their final appearance? Why?

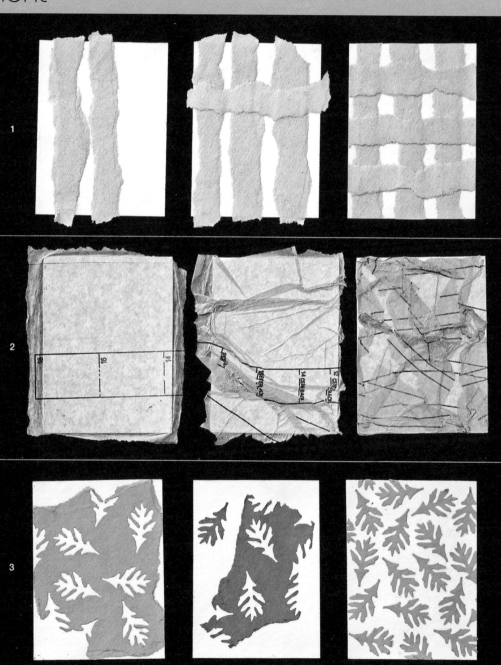

Diffusing Imagery

Materials

- watercolor paper (inexpensive 140 lb. cold press)
- gesso
- matte medium
- 1" (2.5 cm)-wide flat synthetic brushes
- vintage papers, copies or imagery you wish to work with at least as large as your watercolor paper
- small jars for mixing gesso wash and rinsing brushes
- very-fine-grit wet and dry sandpaper

LEARNING OBJECTIVE: To use imagery as a background by distorting and diffusing its impact.

FOOD FOR THOUGHT

- Which kind of imagery was easiest to work with?
- Did the copy bleed? If so, note which one(s).
- Does black-and-white or color diffuse more readily?
- Does the effect of the glossy verses matte paper make a difference in the end result?
- What other kinds of imagery might work?

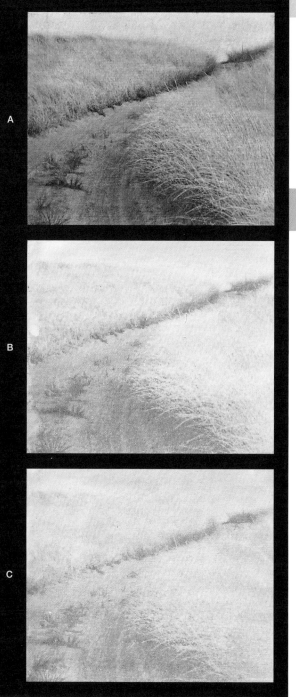

A

B

C

STEP 1: Using matte medium, adhere imagery to watercolor paper. (See A.)

STEP 2: Mix a light wash of gesso and water (40/60) and brush over image. If paper is glossy (such as a magazine or photo), you will have to sand it lightly first to allow adhesion of the gesso. Let dry. (See B.)

STEP 3: Wash two or more times with light gesso wash until imagery is no longer obvious and let dry. (See C.)

Play and Experiment

- Repeat steps 2 and 3, but spray gesso instead of brushing (see example at right).
- Use a color laser photocopy.
- Use a black-and-white laser photocopy.
- Use an ink-jet copy.
- Use an image from a magazine.
- Use a real photograph.
- Use an old map.
- Use a page from an old book, telephone book, or newspaper.

▶ *The samples to the right show the diffusing process on a piece of antique ledger paper.*

LAB 4

Washes

Materials

- watercolor paper (inexpensive 140 lb. cold press)
- gesso
- small, damp sponge
- flat synthetic brushes
- ink
- acrylic or craft paint
- several small jars with lids for mixing washes
- small spray bottle or craft mister
- masking tape

LEARNING OBJECTIVE: To become familiar with creating various washes and their effects.

INSTRUCTIONS

STEP 1: Using water and ink, make several different strength and color variation washes in jars.

STEP 2: Repeat step 1 with water and acrylic paint.

STEP 3: Brush or spray various washes over prepared surfaces (such as those suggested in unit 1 lab 1: Basic Gesso Surface, page 13) or just over watercolor paper if preferred. The effects of the washes will be more evident if your surface is already textured. Using commercially available textured paper is an option for a quick and easy exercise. Paintable wallpaper from your local home center comes in a variety of textures and designs and would be an excellent choice for this exercise.

FOOD FOR THOUGHT

- Which effects yielded most consistent results?
- Which do you prefer, ink or paint? Why?
- Did mixing paint and ink add more interest or make the piece muddy?
- Did lifting the ink work?
- Does paint lift?
- Does ink lift more precisely when paint wash is applied first?
- Did the paper buckle? What could be done to prevent this in the future?

Play and Experiment

EXAMPLE 1: After wash has dried, add second layer of the same color in some but not all areas.

EXAMPLE 2: Apply layer of wash when dry, add second layer of different color in some but not all areas.

EXAMPLE 3: After wash has dried, spray a second layer of different color over entire surface.

EXAMPLE 4: Using a dampened sponge, lift areas of wash, taking advantage of the substrate texture.

EXAMPLE 5: Apply a sprayed wash to dried wash surface with different color.

EXAMPLE 6: Apply a sprayed wash to a dried wash surface and then "buff" with a soft rag.

EXAMPLE 7: Apply a sprayed wash to dried surface, using a deeper shade of the same color.

EXAMPLE 8: Apply a sprayed wash to dried surface with the same color.

EXAMPLE 9: Mix layers of ink and paint when applying; start with paint wash, let dry, and then apply ink wash.

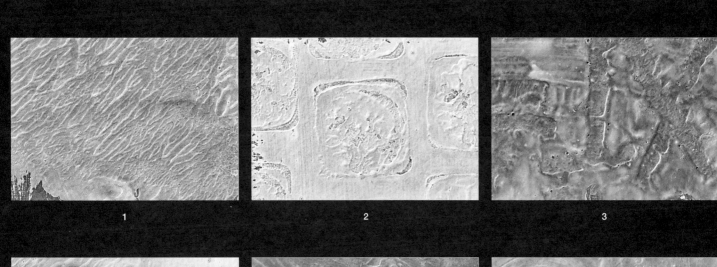

1

2

3

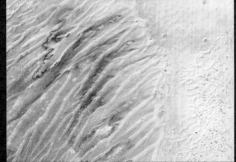

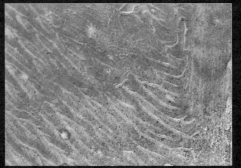

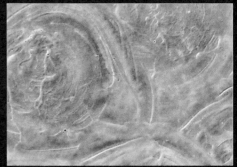

4

5

6

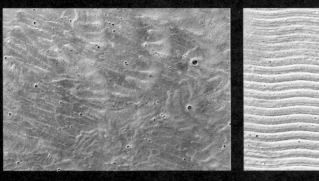

7

8

9

Texture

THERE ARE THOUSANDS of ways to enhance a collage with texture. The following labs are meant as an introduction or a jumping-off point. Rather than trying to control the outcome, allow the materials and methods to direct the work. Liken the process to a child's playing with finger paints; feel the textures in the materials and the results will follow.

The key to success here is not being afraid to fail. If failure is viewed as an opportunity, then the goal to acquire knowledge has been reached.

Be brave, be bold, try anything and everything.

UNIT

2

Artist: Misty Mawn

Corrugated Substrates

- two pieces of corrugated cardboard box (approximately 12" x 16" [30.5 x 40.6 cm])
- gesso
- craft knife
- 1" (2.5 cm)-wide chip brush
- stencil brush
- acrylic paint
- simple stencil such as a circle or square
- walnut or other dark ink

Book created using corrugated cardboard, paint, and wax

LEARNING OBJECTIVE: To incorporate textured recyclables as a background to create depth and interest.

INSTRUCTIONS

STEP 1: Tear the pieces of card board box into eight pieces that are roughly 6" x 8" (15.2 x 20.3 cm).

STEP 2: Try the following techniques for texture on the boards:

- On two pieces, score strips into the top layer and then tear strips of the cardboard surface away from the corrugated middle section along the length or width. (See A.)

- On two pieces, make circles to cut away a specific design, exposing the corrugated middle section. (See B.)

- On two pieces, use various sharp or dull objects to poke holes and tear the cardboard surface, exposing the corrugated middle section. (See C.)

- On two pieces, pull the cardboard surface partially away from the corrugated middle section on about 50 percent of the surface. Tear freely without trying to control the direction. (See D.)

STEP 3: Apply gesso to four of your eight pieces and let dry.

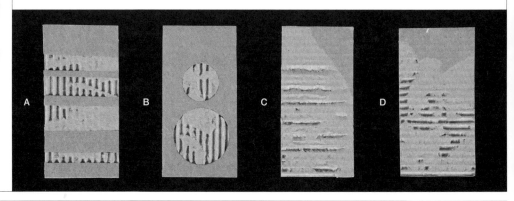

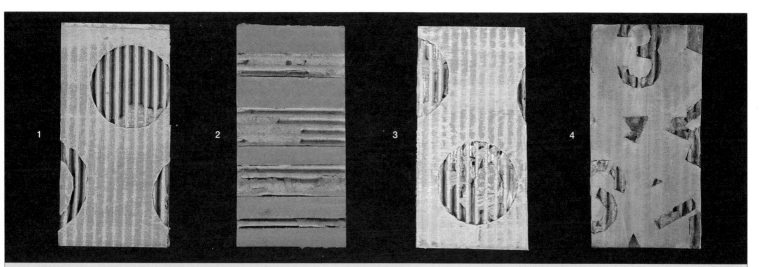

Play and Experiment

On all pieces, both with and without gesso, try the following:

EXAMPLE 1: Paint with full-strength paint in a dark color, then dry-brush to highlight top areas.

EXAMPLE 2: Paint with a wash of a dark color, then dry-brush to highlight top areas with same color full strength.

EXAMPLE 3: Paint with full-strength light color. Let dry. Wash with a dark color.

EXAMPLE 4: Paint with full-strength light color and wash with dark ink.

Torn cardboard collage

FOOD FOR THOUGHT

• Compare the pieces with and without gesso.

• How does a dark highlight differ in effect from a light highlight?

• Would this technique work as a nonsubstrate element? How?

• What are ten ways to change the surface of the corrugated cardboard to create different effects?

• Was ample space left to continue the work?

• How can something be planned to give it meaning without having it appear contrived?

Organics

Materials

- sand
- dried and pressed plant material (herbs work well)
- small whole grains
- feathers
- 1" (2.5 cm)-wide chip brush
- stencil brush
- matte medium
- gesso
- mat board or chipboard cut into 3" x 4" (7.6 x 10.2 cm) pieces
- acrylic paint

3-D collaged shadowbox created from both paper and organic materials

LEARNING OBJECTIVE: To open the door to the possibilities of organic media from the kitchen or garden.

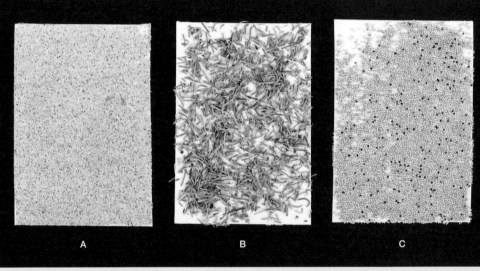

A   B   C

INSTRUCTIONS

STEP 1: Cover board with matte medium.

STEP 2: Sprinkle wet board with sand and shake to cover evenly to edges. (See A.)

STEP 3: Repeat with dried herbs and then with small whole grains. (See B and C.)

STEP 4: Allow to dry, then apply two or three coats of gesso.

STEP 5: Using dried and pressed plant material or feathers and matte medium, create boards that have an allover effect and boards that have just one focal element, referring to examples for ideas.

Play and Experiment

1

2

3

EXAMPLE 1: Apply two coats of dark acrylic paint. Highlight the organic material by dry-brushing a light color on high points.

EXAMPLE 2: Try adding an organic texture to a collage in process rather than as a substrate or background.

EXAMPLE 3: Mix sand with matte medium in small, disposable container and trowel onto surface, forming peaks and valleys. Coat with paint, let dry, and dry-brush metallic paint over high points.

FOOD FOR THOUGHT

• Which materials are you likely to use again? Why?

• Name ten other organic materials to experiment with.

• Does gesso hamper or minimize the effect? Can this be helpful?

• Using matte medium allows the natural material to have more visual impact than just texture. Is this an advantage or a disadvantage?

Fabrics

LEARNING OBJECTIVE: To become familiar with the application of and uses for various common fabrics for creating texture.

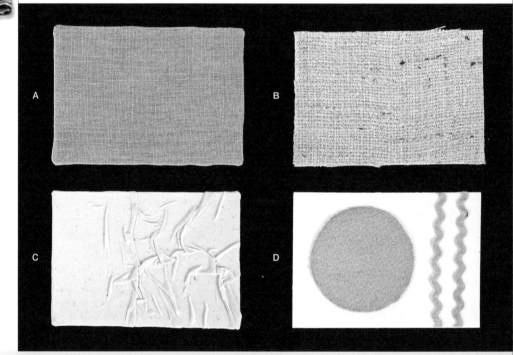

- burlap
- linen
- muslin
- wool
- 1" (2.5 cm)-wide chip brush
- stencil brush
- heavy gel medium
- gesso
- mat board or chipboard cut into 3" x 4" (7.6 x 10.2 cm) pieces
- acrylic paint
- ink

INSTRUCTIONS

STEP 1: Tear and cut various fabrics into small pieces for use on the 3" x 4" (7.6 x 10.2 cm) boards.

STEP 2: Using gel medium, brush both sides of the fabric and surface of the board for

application, working quickly as matte medium has a short open time.

STEP 3: Apply fabric to board as a total background, keeping fabric flat. (See A and B.)

STEP 4: Apply fabric to board as a total background, wrinkling fabric in some places but not others. (See C.)

STEP 5: Apply fabric to board as a focal point. (See D.)

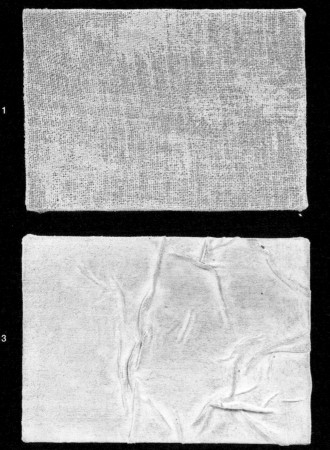

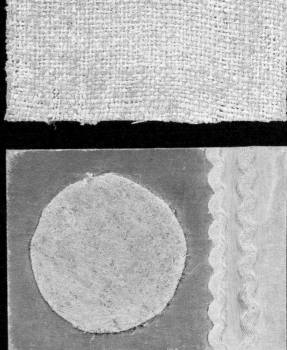

Play and Experiment

EXAMPLE 1: Apply gesso to fabric background completely and wash with acrylic paint.

EXAMPLE 2: Apply gesso to fabric background in some areas but not others and wash with ink.

EXAMPLE 3: Wash fabric with ink wash only.

EXAMPLE 4: Coat fabric with dark acrylic paint and dry-brush light color over raised portions only.

FOOD FOR THOUGHT

- Compare a fabric background to a paper texture background. Does one have more merit than the other, or is it situation-dependent?
- Take a field trip to a fabric store and get inspired.
- Think of five other ways to use fabric in a collage.

Paper

Materials

- cardstock
- tissue paper
- 1" (2.5 cm)-wide chip brush
- stencil brush
- matte medium
- gesso

- mat board or chipboard cut into 3" x 4" (7.6 x 10.2 cm) pieces
- acrylic paint
- craft punches
- scissors
- craft knife

Various textures with gesso and ink wash

LEARNING OBJECTIVE:
To gain new perspectives on the use of paper as a substrate, a background or focal point, and for texture.

Image diffused with tissue paper, then drawn over with pen and tinted

FOOD FOR THOUGHT

- Make a list of all the papers used in this lab. Sort them in order of preference during this experience. Think about why.

- Look around your work space and find ten more types of paper to try in the future.

- Did any of the papers bleed?

- What papers would you never use again? Why?

- What attributes will you look for when choosing papers to work with in the future?

Play and Experiment

STEP 1: Apply paper to board as a border.

STEP 2: Apply paper to board as an all-over background.

STEP 3: Apply paper to board as a raised surface to work on.

STEP 4: Apply tissue paper to board as a total background, wrinkling it up as you go.

STEP 5: Apply gesso to paper background, let dry, then wash with ink.

STEP 6: Paint surface with dark acrylic paint and dry-brush with light color.

STEP 7: Wash surface with ink only, no gesso first.

STEP 8: Apply gesso to surface and wash with acrylic paint.

Gesso

GESSO IS ONE of the most versatile mediums available. It can be used to seal a porous substrate, and it can give you a workable surface where one didn't exist. It can provide texture, color, diffusion, obliteration, cohesiveness, relief layers, and even adhesion.

This is but a short walk into the attributes of gesso. I reach for gesso at least once a day. It's a staple in the studio just as much as milk is in the refrigerator.

Learn its uses, play with it at every opportunity, and sing its praises, for where would we be without it?

UNIT 3

Artist: Shirley Ende-Saxe

Building Layers

Materials

LEARNING OBJECTIVE: To experiment with gesso in building layers and adding dimension to two-dimensional works.

Background substrate of wrinkled tissue and gesso, ink wash. Frog punched from watercolored paper with trowled gesso and paint wash.

- gesso
- 1" (2.5 cm)-wide chip brush
- old credit card
- stencil or piece of cardstock and craft punch
- mat board or chipboard cut into 3" x 4" (7.6 x 10.2 cm) pieces
- acrylic paint
- freezer paper

FOOD FOR THOUGHT

- List ten specific ideas for using gesso in a collage.
- List ten alternative tools for working with the gesso to create texture.
- What other mediums could you use in a similar way?

INSTRUCTIONS

STEP 1: Apply layer of gesso to all of the boards in different ways as suggested below.

STEP 2: Spoon gesso into freezer paper. Using credit card, trowel gesso onto surface of a board, leaving lines and marks much in the same manner that stucco or plaster is applied. (See A.)

STEP 3: Create a stencil (or use an available one) using a piece of cardstock and a craft punch. A circle or square will work just fine. Once the stencil is made, lay it on top of board and apply gesso through opening again by using the credit card to trowel the gesso through the opening. Let set up a few minutes before removing the stencil. (See B and C.)

Play and Experiment

Using examples from the Instructions, apply coat of acrylic paint. Wash with ink or acrylic paint of different color to "pop" texture. (See D, E, and F.)

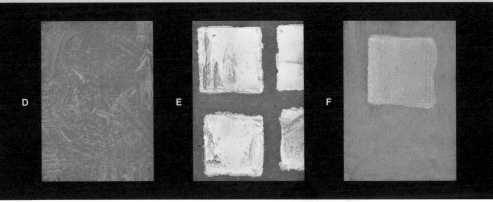

Adding Tints and Color

Materials

- gesso
- acrylic paint
- ink
- tube watercolor
- 1" (2.5 cm)-wide chip brush
- palette knife or tongue depressor
- small containers for mixing (clear works better, but anything will do)
- clean water
- mat board or chipboard cut into 3" x 4" (7.6 x 10.2 cm) pieces
- pencil or pen that will mark on the board clearly

LEARNING OBJECTIVE: To explore methods for tinting gesso using ink and chalk.

FOOD FOR THOUGHT

- How much colorant does it take to make a strongly tinted gesso?
- Is it better to add gesso to colorant or colorant to gesso? Why?

Play and Experiment

- Try combining paint and ink mixtures.
- Try combining paint and pastel mixtures.
- Apply one color and type; let dry. Now apply second coat over top with different color and allow some of original to come through or scrape away part of second coat.

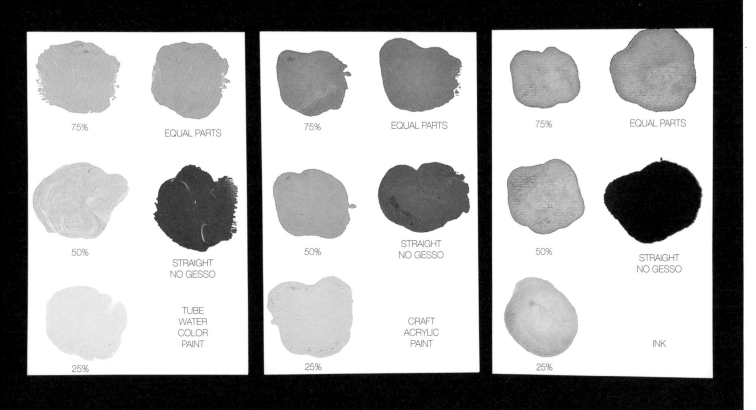

75%   EQUAL PARTS

50%   STRAIGHT NO GESSO

25%   TUBE WATER COLOR PAINT

75%   EQUAL PARTS

50%   STRAIGHT NO GESSO

25%   CRAFT ACRYLIC PAINT

75%   EQUAL PARTS

50%   STRAIGHT NO GESSO

25%   INK

INSTRUCTIONS

STEP 1: Spoon small amount of gesso into mixing container.

STEP 2: Starting with the first container, add a little watercolor paint and mix thoroughly. Brush a little of the mixture onto the board, making a "sample." Mark the sample with ratio of gesso to paint. (See example 25%.)

STEP 3: Add more paint and mix again. Repeat sample and make notation. (See example 50%.)

STEP 4: Repeat a third time. (See example 75%.)

STEP 5: Repeat a fourth time. (See example equal parts.)

STEP 6: Put a sample of straight paint for comparison on the board. (See example straight no gesso.)

STEP 7: Begin a new board. This time, repeat above process, using acrylic paint in place of watercolor paint.

STEP 8: Begin a new board. This time, repeat above process, using inks.

Sanding Back

- gesso
- mat board or chipboard cut into 3" x 4" (7.6 x 10.2 cm) pieces
- 1" (2.5 cm)-wide chip brush
- lightweight dry and wet sandpaper
- images (copies, black-and-white or color, magazine clippings, etc.)
- matte medium

LEARNING OBJECTIVE: To explore methods for deconstructing images using gesso and sandpaper as primary medium.

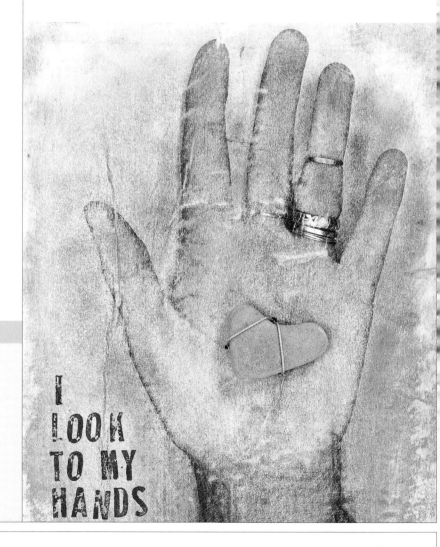

FOOD FOR THOUGHT

- Does this method work well for a piece in process? Why or why not? When would it and when wouldn't it?
- Which works better, dry or wet sanding? Why?
- List ten types of images to try again with in the future.
- List five other mediums to use in place of gesso for this method.

INSTRUCTIONS

STEP 1: Prepare boards: Cut to fit and adhere an image or copy (or use a collage already in process) to boards, using matte medium. Allow to dry.

STEP 2: Coat boards with gesso to varying degrees. All boards should have imagery showing through to some extent—some more, some less. (See A, B, and C.)

STEP 3: Once dry, choose a board and begin to sand back the gesso to reveal the imagery underneath.

STEP 4: Repeat until all boards have been sanded.

STEP 5: Make sure to try both dry and wet sandpaper and mark the boards accordingly.

Play and Experiment

EXAMPLE 1: Cover just a portion of the entire board to create "mystery" area or a place where you could add another image or text.

EXAMPLE 2: Sand back selected areas to focus on the image and blur just the background.

EXAMPLE 3: Try coating an image completely with a gesso wash so that it is mostly obliterated and then sand it back to create age and wear.

Overprinting

- gesso
- household sponge cut into small pieces
- mat board cut into 3" x 4" (7.6 x 10.2 cm) pieces
- images (copies, black-and-white or color, magazine clippings, etc.)
- matte medium
- chip brush
- things to print with (stamps, household objects, etc.)
- clean water

LEARNING OBJECTIVE: To discover diverse ways of using tinted gesso for overprinting.

INSTRUCTIONS

STEP 1: Cut boards to fit and adhere an image or copy (or use a collage already in process that has hit the scrap pile) to boards using matte medium. Allow to dry.

STEP 2: Apply gesso to printing surface, referring to examples for guidance and ideas.

1

2

3

4

Play and Experiment

EXAMPLE 1: Sponge tinted gesso in contrasting color over edges of work.

EXAMPLE 2: Use a combination of sponging and printing with a rubber stamp.

EXAMPLE 3: Apply a wash of tinted gesso over a small piece of the imagery to set it apart.

EXAMPLE 4: Create a light wash of tinted gesso and diffuse entire image to push it back.

FOOD FOR THOUGHT

- How does the printed image or word accentuate the underlying imagery?

- List ten items visually available at this moment that could be used to print with.

- Pull out previous work and think about how using overprinting could have enhanced the piece. Make notes and try it again.

Color

AT SOME POINT DURING our education we have all been introduced to color theory, but a little review and color calisthenics once in awhile never hurts anyone.

The following labs should be viewed as a reintroduction to the basics. Starting with a basic color wheel to create a common ground for the exploration to continue, the labs will move on to more specific areas of the effects of color.

Color is one of the major contributors in a collage. It can set the mood, create an impact, relax the viewer, or excite the viewer. Color choices are based on many concepts but largely chosen to specifically communicate an idea or thought from creator to viewer. Consider this exploration into the wonderful world of color a step back into the past and forward into the work.

UNIT

4

deeply buried

Artist: Katie Kendrick

Basic Theory

Materials

- one piece of inexpensive watercolor paper 7" x 7" (17.8 x 17.8 cm)
- one piece of inexpensive watercolor paper cut into twelve 3" x 4" (7.6 x 10.2 cm) rectangles
- red, blue, and yellow acrylic or watercolor paint
- small paintbrush
- clean water
- pencil
- compass
- protractor
- ruler

LEARNING OBJECTIVE: To become familiar with or revisit the basics of color theory and how color affects the work, and to create a color wheel and color chips to build the visual toolbox.

INSTRUCTIONS

STEP 1: Using the compass, draw a circle on the piece of watercolor paper.

STEP 2: Find the center and carefully divide the circle into quarters, using the ruler.

STEP 3: Divide the quarters again using the protractor so that the circle contains twelve "slices" in total. Think of the twelve sections as if they were hours on a clock and paint as follows: From twelve to one paint yellow. From four to five paint red. From eight to nine paint blue. These are your primary colors.

STEP 4: Begin to mix the secondary colors (colors formed by mixing two primary colors). They will be green (equal parts yellow and blue), orange (equal parts yellow and red), and violet (equal parts blue and red). Paint as follows: Green is painted from ten to eleven, orange is painted from two to three, and violet is painted from six to seven.

STEP 5: Begin to mix the tertiary colors (colors formed by mixing a primary color with a secondary color). Mix equal parts of the two colors and paint as follows: Red and orange to make red-orange and paint from three to four. Yellow and orange to make yellow-orange and paint from one to two. Red and violet to make red-violet and paint from five to six. Violet and blue to make blue-violet and paint from seven to eight. Blue and green to make blue-green and paint from nine to ten. Green and yellow to make green-yellow and paint from eleven to twelve.

Play and Experiment

- Using the 3" x 4" (7.6 x 10.2 cm) pieces, begin to explore the color relationships by first drawing small squares in the center of your piece. Paint four of the squares blue.

- Paint the surrounding area of each one as follows: one with black, one with white, and the two with the other two primary colors. (See examples above.)

- Repeat with yellow.

- Repeat with red.

- Compare the color chips and the effect of the surrounding colors. Take note of which combinations push the focus color back and which ones make it pop.

- Think about ways to use this in your work.

Emotional Impact

Materials

- inexpensive watercolor paper (140 lb. cold press or anything available)
- magazines with colorful photos
- small paintbrush
- clean water
- compass
- protractor
- pencil
- ruler
- glue stick

LEARNING OBJECTIVE: To explore the effects of color on emotional senses.

Play and Experiment

- With the hot color wheel in visual range, write a list of words that come to mind for at least three minutes. Don't think too much, don't force it, just feel it and write it.
- Repeat with the cool color wheel.

Here, both photos show the same basic imagery, but the backgrounds on which they sit clearly state a different message. On the left, the background uses a complementary color that calms down the hot colors of the drinks and makes the viewer feel enticed by its refreshing qualities. In contrast, the photo on the right uses the same colors in the background to excite the viewer and send a completely different message.

FOOD FOR THOUGHT

- Examine the word lists generated by the automatic writing and compare it to the notes taken while the wheels were being created.
- Identify the emotions connected to the colors and make notes on your wheels for future reference.

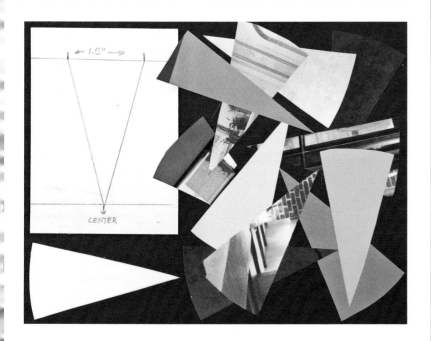

INSTRUCTIONS

STEP 1: Cull through magazines and pull out photos with hot colors. Don't think too much—just tear and make a pile.

STEP 2: Using the template (see left), cut out pie shapes of color. They do not have to be solid color, just predominately the colors you are looking for.

STEP 3: Create a color wheel using only hot colors (yellows, oranges, and reds) out of your pie shapes.

STEP 4: While you are working on the color wheel, make notes about how you are feeling as you are working with the colors.

STEP 5: Repeat and make a cool color wheel (blues, greens, and violets).

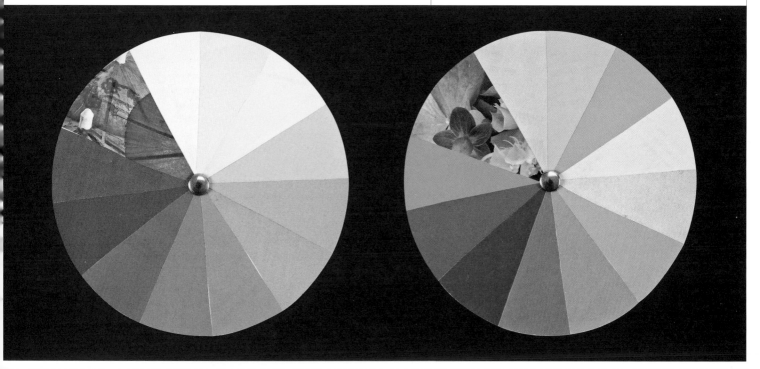

LAB 15

The Personal Palette

Materials

- inexpensive watercolor paper (140 lb. cold press or anything available)
- magazines with colorful photos
- scissors
- glue stick
- pencil

LEARNING OBJECTIVE: To find personal preferences in color while working.

FOOD FOR THOUGHT

- Identify the colors you are most comfortable working with.

- Identify those colors that you tend to avoid.

- Give thought to your favorite colors and create your "dream palette." Make notes on why you lean towards those colors.

- Give thought to the colors you shy away from and make notes on why you avoid them and why you shouldn't.

- What was the single most important thing you learned about your color choices?

INSTRUCTIONS

STEP 1: Cull through the magazines and tear out photos with colors that appeal to you. Do *not* think hard about choices; if you like the color, tear it out and make a pile.

STEP 2: Make a pile of watercolor paper rectangles for the base of the color chips.

STEP 3: Using the glue stick, glue the chip bases to the backs of the photos and trim.

STEP 4: Punch holes at the top (you can even add eyelets to aid in longevity) and keep the color chips handy for inspiration.

STEP 5: Do this exercise now and again and add to the grouping.

Play and Experiment

- Create a list of the colors regularly used in your work.
- Compare with the completed color chips.
- Create a list of the colors that draw your eye in the work of others.
- Create a list of the colors used to decorate the personal spaces in home, office, and studio.
- Identify the six colors that come up most frequently on these lists.

Shadow and Light

Materials

- inexpensive watercolor paper (140 lb. cold press or anything available)
- black acrylic paint
- white acrylic paint
- one primary color of acrylic paint
- small paintbrush
- clean water
- pencil
- compass
- ruler

LEARNING OBJECTIVE: To practice scales and reinforce value and hue definitions, and to help the artist understand the nature of value concerning color by removing the hue and working only with the value.

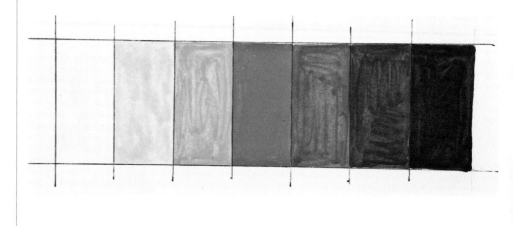

INSTRUCTIONS

STEP 1: Create a value bar as follows:

STEP 2: Draw a 7" (17.8 cm)-wide x 2" (5.1 cm)-tall rectangle on the watercolor paper.

STEP 3: Divide the rectangle into seven equal segments.

STEP 4: Paint the rectangle on the far right black.

STEP 5: Paint the rectangle on the far left white.

STEP 6: Mix equal parts of black and white and paint the middle segment the resulting gray.

STEP 7: Divide remaining gray mix into two parts.

STEP 8: On the white side, mix equal parts of gray mix and white, and paint in segment directly to the left of the gray mix in center.

STEP 9: Using gray-white mix, add equal parts white to lighten once more and paint in last open segment on left.

STEP 10: Repeat steps for black side of value bar.

Play and Experiment

- Choose a primary color and create a hue bar with primary and white, and then repeat one with primary color and black.

- Choose a secondary color and create a hue bar with secondary and white, and then repeat with secondary color and black.

- Choose a tertiary color and create a hue bar with tertiary and white, and then repeat with tertiary color and black.

- Draw a simple image such as an apple or a pear and use only black and white and shades of gray to paint in only the values of what the eye sees.

FOOD FOR THOUGHT

- What values are dulled by white? Black?

- What values are pumped up by white? Black?

- Think about how changing the value of a color impacts the viewer and the concept the work is trying to convey.

- How does changing the value of a hue affect communication?

Surface Design

SURFACE DESIGN introduces depth and character to work by using a wide range of techniques: printing, patterns, stencils, masks, stamps, and more. One of the most important aspects of surface design is that it offers ways to make your designs more personal. Whether you are carving images, creating stencils or masks, or mark making, you are putting yourself immediately but not obviously into the work.

UNIT

5

Artist: Anne Bagby

Carving Personal Images

Materials

- Mars Carving Block (or similar product)
- lino tools and sharp craft knife for cutting into carving block
- tracing paper
- pencil
- fabric, wrapping paper, or image to work from
- water-soluble printing inks, commercial ink pads, or acrylic paints
- soft brayer (if using printing inks or acrylic paint, for ease of application)

LEARNING OBJECTIVE: To become comfortable with creating personal images and patterns from readily available sources.

FOOD FOR THOUGHT

- Do bolder patterns work better than more intricate patterns?
- How does ink differ from paint in the result?
- How does printing ink and ink from an ink pad differ in result?
- Do you have to wait for layers to dry before overprinting?
- Which media was most comfortable to work with?

Play and Experiment

- Print repeat patterns. Try as many variations as the particular block will allow. Samples 1 and 2 show the same stamp printed two ways.

- Overprint with different colors. Sample 3 shows the same stamp background with a different stamp overprinting with white.

INSTRUCTIONS

STEP 1: Working directly from fabric, paper, or image, trace portions of the design that are appealing. Make effort to not copy directly but to interpret the image.

STEP 2: Turn tracing paper pencil side down onto surface of carving block and burnish with thumbnail or bowl of spoon.

STEP 3: Carve away areas that are not to be printed, leaving printed area raised. (Hint: Place carving block on piece of tracing paper to allow for easier movement while carving. Move the block more than you move the cutting tool.)

STEP 4: Rinse with water and blot dry.

STEP 5: Once the block is complete, use it to print with. Start with one basic print at a time and get comfortable with loading the chosen media onto the block.

Masks and Stencils

- oak tag (manila file folder or cardstock)
- cutting surface and craft knife
- old magazines or images for cutting shapes
- ruler
- pencil
- glue stick
- stencil brush
- acrylic paint
- substrate of choice (watercolor paper, cardstock, mat board, etc.) with or without background completed

LEARNING OBJECTIVE: To explore positive and negative shapes, using masks and stencils.

FOOD FOR THOUGHT

- List ten ways to use a mask or stencil.
- Make a list of shapes and form "basics" to use in your work to build a supply of stencils and masks.
- Which lends itself better to creating a positive space? Why?
- Consider other materials to use as a ready-made stencil and make a list (e.g., sequin waste and cardboard alphabet and number stencils).

INSTRUCTIONS

STEP 1: Choose an image or shape to work with from magazine or image stash. Cut it out and glue to oak tag or cardstock. (See A.)

STEP 2: Using a craft knife, carefully cut out the shape around all edges. (See B.) Pop the shape out of the larger form. The shape removed is the mask and the larger form is the stencil. Both positive and negative spaces have been created for use.

STEP 3: Noting the important detail on the image of the mask, cut shapes to define important areas of detail. (See C.)

Play and Experiment

- Load the stencil brush with very little paint making sure to wipe off any excess paint. This is referred to as a dry-brush technique.

- Using the stencil, create a shape.

- Using the mask, create shadows around the stenciled shape.

- Use the stencil on an old piece of work to add a new detail.

- Use only part of the stencil on a piece.

- Once initial stenciling is completed, digitize the piece and play with different filters to see how the image changes.

Collage sample using stencil and mask

Digital version of collage using stencil and mask

LAB 19 Stamping and Mark Making

Materials

- commercially available sponges, brayers, and stamps (items from the children's art section at your craft store work well)
- acrylic paint
- text-weight paper
- water for rinsing

LEARNING OBJECTIVE: To experiment with the results of commercially available tools for mark making and stamping.

FOOD FOR THOUGHT

- Did favorite tools keep appealing to you? Why?
- How much effect on the outcome did the colors have versus the results of the tools?
- Think about what is available in your home that you could work with. Make a list and go find them!

INSTRUCTIONS

STEP 1: Create a wash of several different colors of acrylic paint and coat five to ten pieces of paper with each color. Let dry.

STEP 2: Using waxed paper or some kind of palette, spread acrylic paint out in small sections to enable the tools to run through or be loaded evenly.

STEP 3: Begin to play with the tools in a random fashion and just make designs.

STEP 4: Don't stress; just play.

Play and Experiment

- Try different color combinations using the same tools and patterns.

- Make different patterns with the same tool. How many ways can it work?

- Take a trip to the hardware store, the paint store, and the art supply store . . . investigate what else is out there for use and create a wish list.

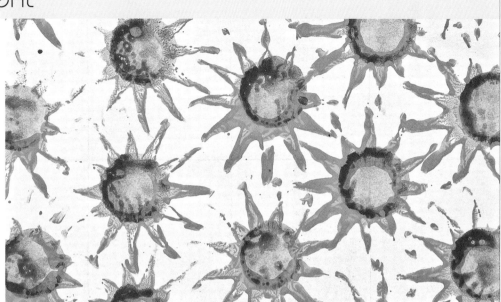

Book covers made from stamped papers

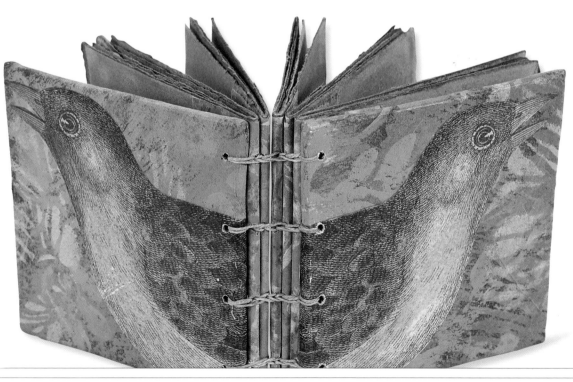

Making Personal Tools

- old plastic lids (such as a margarine lid)
- wooden blocks
- packaging foam
- rug slip mats
- old place mats
- corks
- toothbrush
- plastic wrap
- string
- acrylic paint
- text-weight paper and/or cardstock

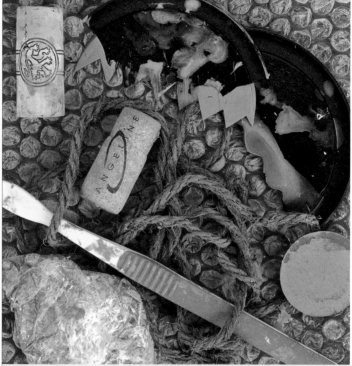

LEARNING OBJECTIVE: To discover what tools are close at hand and how they will work.

INSTRUCTIONS

STEP 1: Cut plastic lids in half and make a decorative edge. (See example above.)

STEP 2: Crumple up plastic wrap into small ball.

STEP 3: Cut pieces of place mat, packing foam, and rug mat and adhere to wooden blocks to make stamps (blocks shown on page 59).

STEP 4: Lay out acrylic paints in a variety of colors on a palette to dip the tools into.

STEP 5: Begin to play and print, making repeating patterns on the papers.

Play and Experiment

- Don't let paint dry before adding another layer, to allow them to mix.

- Water down some of the paint to make it flow more.

- Spatter with the toothbrush by running thumb over the top of it when loaded with paint.

FOOD FOR THOUGHT

- Which tools were most effective? Why?

- Which tools were the most fun to use? Why?

- List ten other items you can think of to gather and play with next time.

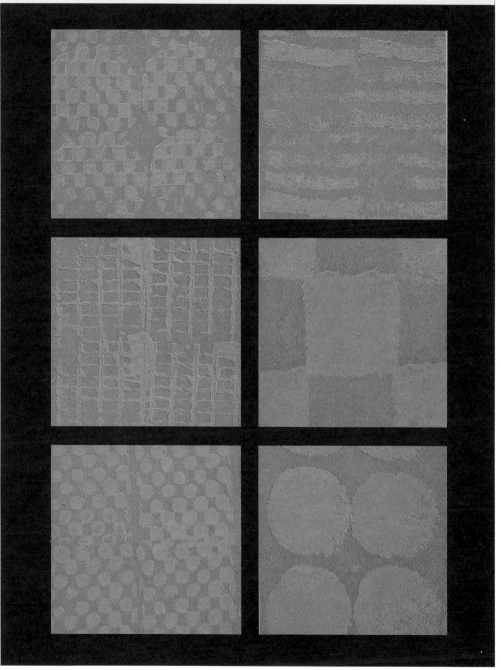

21 LAB

Glazing

Materials

- matte medium
- acrylic paint (brown and white)
- ink
- substrate with finished work or background texture
- graining combs, sponges, rollers, and things to stamp with into the glaze

LEARNING OBJECTIVE: To become familiar with the basics of glaze and how it can change the surface appearance.

INSTRUCTIONS

Prepare the substrate by applying a thin sealer coat of matte medium. Let dry. Repeat.

STEP 1: To make a glaze, mix brown paint and matte medium in 40/60 proportions. Cover surface and then wipe.

STEP 2: Repeat, using a wash of white acrylic paint mixed with water in 40/60 proportions. Do not wipe.

STEP 3: Mix ink (choosing a color already present in the piece) with matte medium, using the same ratio as with the brown paint. Coat surface of a third piece and wipe back.

Collage house with glazed surface

1

2

3

Play and Experiment

- Try a piece without wiping back the glaze but in place of that, pull surface design tools through the glaze.

- Have a piece of work in the discard pile that the colors are just not working in? Pull it out, make an ink glaze using one of the colors in the piece, and glaze it.

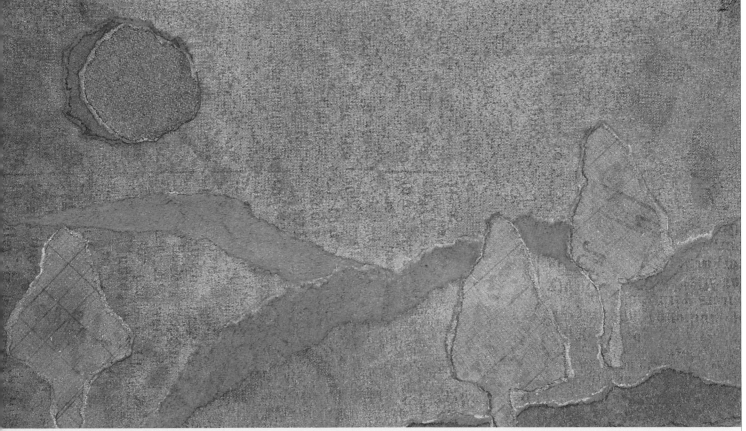

FOOD FOR THOUGHT

- How do different glazes/patterns change the same piece?

- Does glazing with a color from your collage unify the piece more effectively than using, say, a white or brown glaze? What are the differences?

- Are bold patterns more or less effective in a glaze?

- How do progressive coats of sealer affect the glaze surface?

Line and Form

PAUL KLEE ONCE SAID that drawing is like "taking a line for a walk." Lines and forms can be used together and separately to create artistic compositions. These exercises will help explore these concepts and how they can be used to enrich your work.

UNIT

6

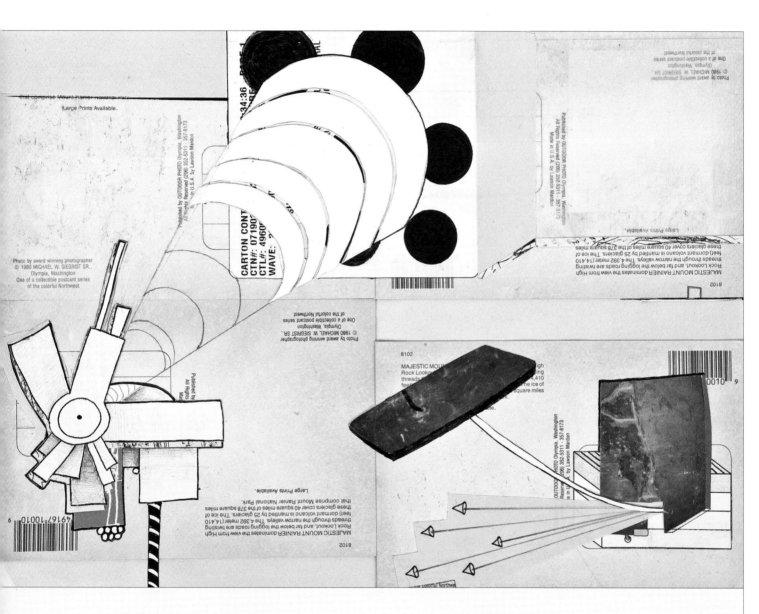

Artist: Laura Kinney

Basic Geometry

Materials

- imagery to work with (choose four or five related images in different sizes)
- pencil
- watercolor paper
- ruler
- compass
- colored cardstock
- glue stick

LEARNING OBJECTIVE: To explore the basics of form and shape and how they affect composition.

Play and Experiment

- Create a series of geometric shapes and assemble them into a composition.
- Try the composition in two different ways.
- Compare the results.

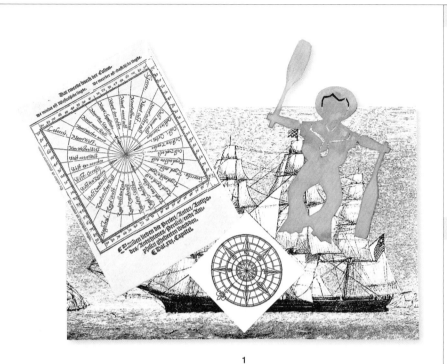

1

STEP 1: Reduce each of your image shapes to their basic geometry.

STEP 2: Play with the arrangements of the geometric shapes on the background until the arrangement is pleasing to the eye.

STEP 3: Complete the collage using real imagery.

FOOD FOR THOUGHT

- Which combinations have the most visual impact?
- What sinks into the background?
- What comes to the foreground?

2

3

Take a Line for a Walk

Materials

- black roller ball or felt-tip pen
- white paper (copy paper will work just fine)
- a timer
- something to draw

LEARNING OBJECTIVE: To become more comfortable with using pens and pencils as a way to communicate in your work through continued practice.

INSTRUCTIONS

STEP 1: Choose something to draw. It shouldn't be too simple. Choose a landscape or still life or human form or a pet. Feel free to work from a photo.

STEP 2: Set the timer for fifteen minutes and start drawing your subject.

STEP 3: Start by defining the overall look or content of your subject. Work large in broad movements to capture the form and shape of your subject. (See A.)

STEP 4: Spend the next five minutes moving closer to the detail by shading the darker areas with lines and making the lighter areas stand out. (See B.)

STEP 5: Spend the final five minutes adding detail. (See C.)

STEP 6: Put your pen down when the timer rings.

Artist: Lowell Shay

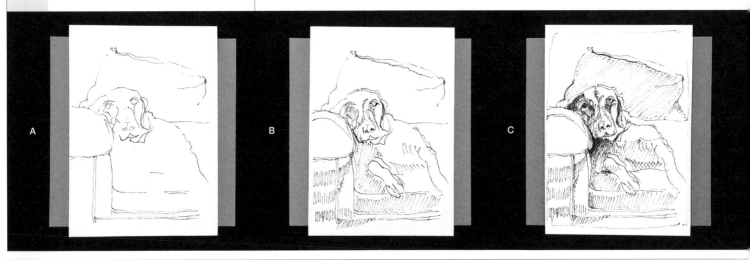

A   B   C

Play and Experiment

- Draw the same subject every day for a week.
- Draw the same subject twice, the second time without lifting your pen.
- Draw the subject without looking down at your paper.
- Draw with pencil.
- Draw with pastel or charcoal.

Artist's self portrait at 16 from photo

FOOD FOR THOUGHT

- Did your drawings improve when drawn repeatedly?
- How did different drawing tools affect the outcome?
- Which did you prefer?

Found in Nature

- photograph or image to work from
- text-weight paper
- pencil
- copy machine (useful but not necessary)
- decorated paper (your own or commercial scrapbooking paper)
- glue stick

LEARNING OBJECTIVE: To find inspiration in objects in the environment and everyday life.

INSTRUCTIONS

STEP 1: Using a pencil, lightly outline (or trace) on text-weight paper the basic form and details of your image. (See A.)

STEP 2: Using this line drawing as a template, cut or tear out just the overall shape of your subject to form the background. (See B.)

STEP 3: Using the basic forms from your line drawing, continue to cut or tear out the "details" from different papers to complete the shape. (See C.)

STEP 4: Make copies of the resulting image in different sizes to play with. (See D, opposite page.) Use a transparency if you want to reverse the image.

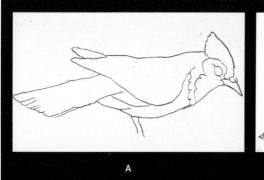

A

B

C

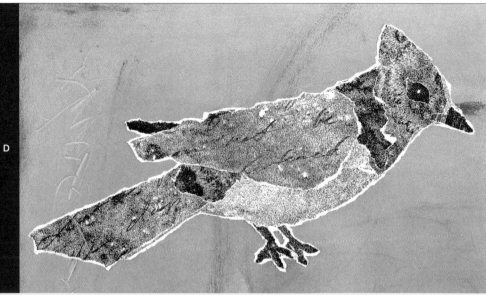

D

- How does removing color from the work change its appearance?

- Is there a preference for cut or torn edges? Why?

- Which is harder, working from real life or working from a photograph without tracing?

Play and Experiment

- Use the resulting image in a collage.

- Using the same method, create a landscape or seascape.

- Using a photograph, create a portrait with this method.

- Get brave and try a portrait from a real model.

- Make sure to try cutting and tearing your edges.

- assorted papers
- watercolor paper or prepared substrate of choice
- imagery
- pencils and/or pens
- glue stick
- scissors or craft knife

LEARNING OBJECTIVE: To find balance and connectivity in composition by connecting the shapes and forms.

Play and Experiment

- Take a piece from the scrap pile and start over, using the instructions to find ways to improve it.
- Make a black-and-white copy of a piece. Work the pieces at the same time but add no color to the black-and-white piece, just the line or forms that are added should be the same. Compare the two to review how the color enhances or distracts from the work.

FOOD FOR THOUGHT

- Set the pairs of collages together where you can see them for a few days. Be sure it is someplace where you will walk by them several times a day.
- What stands out the most?
- What works? What doesn't?
- Does the mark making and drawing pull the forms together or push them away from one another?
- What are the most useful and interesting observations made?

INSTRUCTIONS

STEP 1: Prepare a simple collage and color copy it several times. Also make one black-and-white copy. (See A.)

STEP 2: Turn one of the two upside down. Using mark making or drawing, work through each of the compositions separately, uniting the forms and imagery. (See B.)

STEP 3: Change the orientation of the piece. Using mark making or drawing, work through each of the compositions separately, uniting the forms and imagery. (See C.)

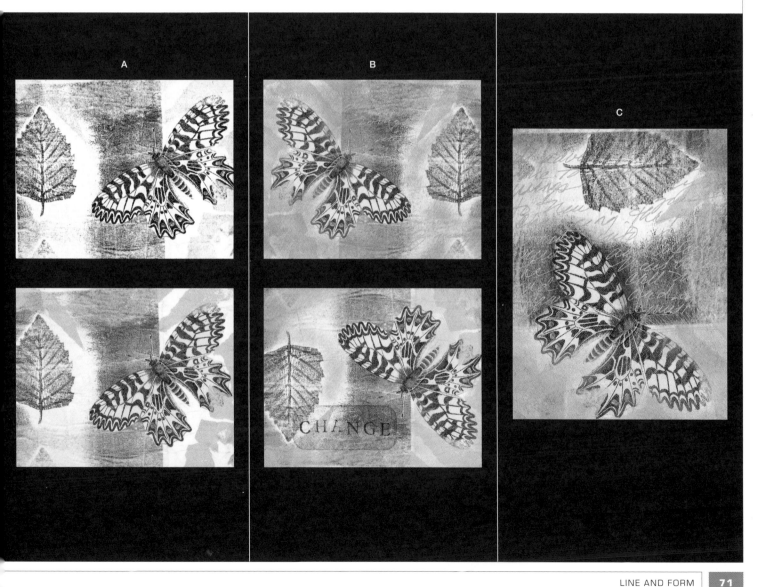

A

B

C

Papers

PAPER PLAYS ONE of the most important roles in a collage. It's the sugar in the cake or the tea in the hot water. Paper can contribute to many aspects of a collage. It can create a textured background, or be painted, stamped, printed, and completely morphed into something it wasn't to add richness and depth of form and color. It can be just a spot of color in the right place, or it can be the key element or focal point of your work.

UNIT 7

Artist: Jen Goff

26

Traditional

- small notebook or journal and pen
- books on collage and collage artists (either from your own collection or the library; try to choose from artists that you are both familiar with and unfamiliar with)
- copier, scanner, or camera to take photos for your notes

LEARNING OBJECTIVE: To take a look at the work of traditional collage artists and use them as inspiration for new works.

INSTRUCTIONS

STEP 1: Get comfortable, sit down, and start paging through the books, taking special notice of what types of papers different artists use and how they use them.

STEP 2: If you can, make copies, scan, or photograph (keeping in mind this is for personal use only) those works that have used papers in interesting ways.

STEP 3: Note the kind of papers you see and how they are used.

STEP 4: Note what you might use a particular paper for that you hadn't thought of before.

STEP 5: Note what papers are used most often.

COLLAGE LAB

Play and Experiment

- Find some of the papers that you have discovered in your research and try working with them.

- Using the old method of "copying the masters," copy a finished piece as best you can.

- Using the style of someone's work that appeals to you, create your own collage in their style.

Author's work emulating Fred Otnes

FOOD FOR THOUGHT

- Are there papers that you found were used by many artists many times?

- What was it about the papers they chose and how they chose them that appealed to you?

- Was copying someone's finished work without step-by-step instructions harder or easier than you thought?

- How difficult is it to copy someone's style but find yourself in the work and make it your own? How did you accomplish this?

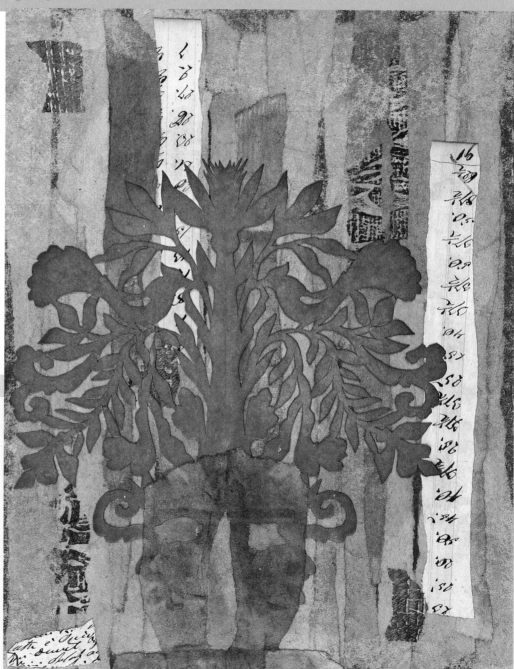

Handmade

LEARNING OBJECTIVE: To investigate handmade papers.

- papermaking kit, which should include a deckle, mold, and pulp material as well as instructions

  or

- Plan a field trip to a paper store and purchase at least five different sheets of handmade paper.

FOOD FOR THOUGHT

- Which papers would you choose to work with again? Why?
- What attributes would you look for when shopping for papers now?
- What were your favorite and least favorite papers, and why?
- Which papers took surface design or printing well?
- Think about keeping a journal with samples of your favorites and notes on how you made them.

INSTRUCTIONS

STEP 1: If the option to make paper was chosen, follow the kit instructions and make paper.

Play and Experiment

If you purchased your paper, try the following hand-embellishing techniques:

EXAMPLE 1: Stamp with acrylic and let dry. Stamp again with ink.

EXAMPLE 2: Paint surface with acrylic paint, let dry, then coat with ink. Pull brush through wet ink and remove in some areas.

EXAMPLE 3: Spray surface with both paint and ink.

EXAMPLE 4: Spray and spatter surface with both paint and ink.

EXAMPLE 5: Stamp with two different colors of ink.

EXAMPLE 6: Spatter with ink.

EXAMPLE 7: Spatter with paint and let dry. Stamp with ink and then mist lightly with water when almost dry.

EXAMPLE 8: Stamp with acrylic paint and while still wet, stamp with ink.

EXAMPLE 9: Stamp with acrylic paint and while still wet, stamp with ink, then mist lightly with water when almost dry.

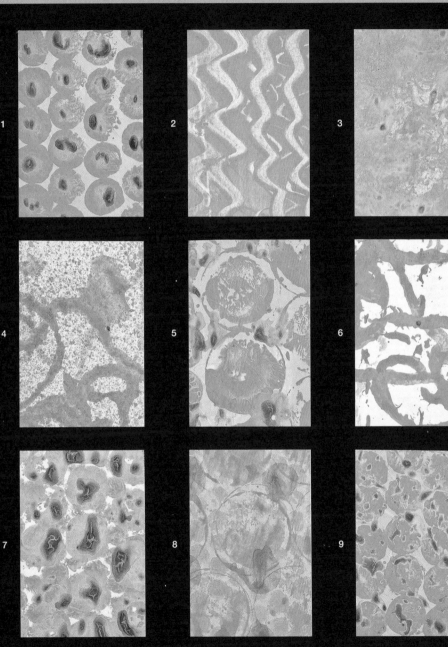

Commercial

- scrapbooking paper, wrapping paper, or even magazine imagery
- a copy machine that reduces and enlarges (this may require a field trip)
- inks
- acrylic paints
- chip brush

LEARNING OBJECTIVE: To explore ways to make commercially produced paper more personal.

INSTRUCTIONS

STEP 1: Make black-and-white copies from your chosen papers, enlarging and reducing.

STEP 2: Bring them back to your work space and continue to make experimental compositions.

FOOD FOR THOUGHT

- How have your choices changed over the course of three or four times of doing this exercise?
- Do you have colors that you always gravitate toward? If yes, why?
- Is it harder to see things you don't like or things you do when searching?

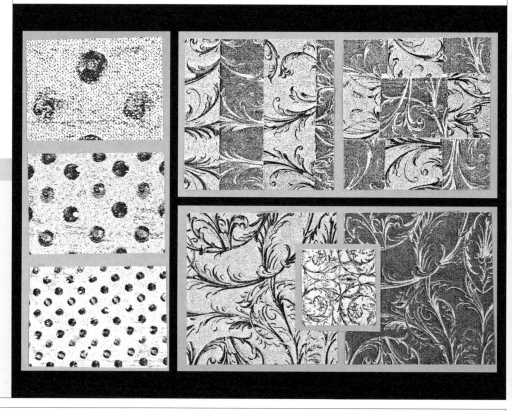

Play and Experiment

- Using ink and acrylic paint washes, color the copies you've made to create paper.

- Relate color choices to papers of same pattern but different sizes to use together.

- Try inverting the copy to produce a negative version of the print before colorizing.

Reclaimed

- found papers (magazines, junk mail, fliers, worn and weathered scraps found on the ground)
- inks
- acrylic paints
- gesso
- pencil
- watercolor paper or substrates of choice
- craft knife and cutting surface
- glue stick and/or matte medium

LEARNING OBJECTIVE: To become more aware of the paper resources in our everyday lives.

Journal made from recycled book and papers; used to keep samples and notes about found and recycled papers of interest

INSTRUCTIONS

STEP 1: Collect ten different types of paper from your household.

STEP 2: Collect scrap paper from your studio or work space.

STEP 3: Take a walk through your town or neighborhood shopping area and collect free paper (fliers, newsletters, etc.).

STEP 4: Choose several different papers from your stash.

STEP 5: Cut or tear at least ten small rectangles from each piece to work with.

STEP 6: Create a journal of samples of different papers and jot down notes about what appeals to you, where you found it, and methods that should be tried using it.

Play and Experiment

- Use your swaps to create a collage.
- Try using the same paper several different ways, and compare results.

FOOD FOR THOUGHT

- How has your awareness of readily available paper changed?
- What types of papers draw the eye?
- Do images or print capture your attention first?
- Where did you find a paper resource where you least expected it?
- What paper surprised you the most, and why?

Specialty

- tissue paper (white and several colors)
- lace paper (available in fine art supply stores)
- matte medium
- watercolor paper or substrate of choice, previous collage work or image to work over
- chip brush

LEARNING OBJECTIVE: To explore how specialty papers can enhance the work.

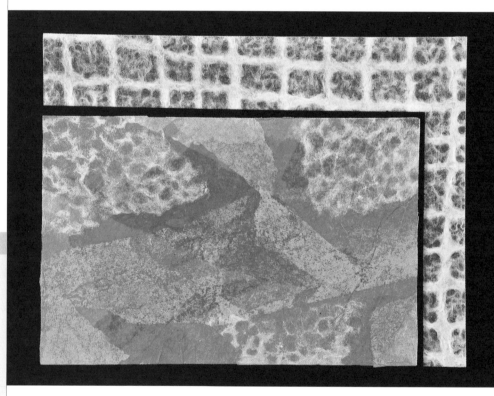

FOOD FOR THOUGHT

- Does the amount of matte medium affect how much the specialty paper "melts"?
- How does color in the tissue change the effect?
- What happens when you layer two or more pieces of tissue over one another? How can that work to your advantage?
- How can that work to your disadvantage?
- What other types of thin paper could be used in the same manner?

Two common and fun specialty papers are tissue and lace. Both melt when used with matte medium, so they lend an air of transparency while building layers. It's a wonderful combination. Tissue needs to be tested as many of the less expensive tissues will bleed color. This could actually be used to an advantage, but best to test first to be sure it's what you want. Lace paper is a little more difficult to find, but most fine art supply stores carry several affordable varieties.

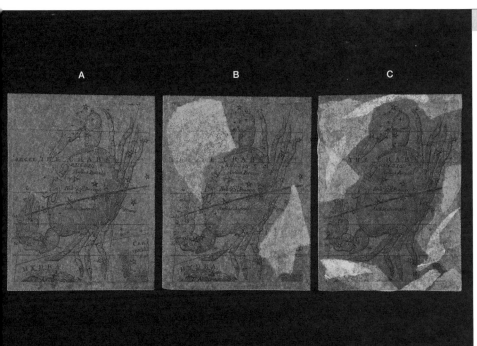

A B C

INSTRUCTIONS

STEP 1: Coat the background of your substrate with a light coat of matte medium.

STEP 2: Tear a piece of colored tissue large enough to cover the work completely and lay down over piece.

STEP 3: Coat with a light coat of matte medium to blend tissue onto image. (See A.)

STEP 4: Tear small pieces of a lighter color of tissue and lay over wetted area and apply another thin coat of matte medium over the top, smoothing down and effectively "melting" the tissue over the previous color. (See B.)

STEP 5: Repeat step 4 with a third color. Let dry. (See C.)

Play and Experiment

- Cover entire piece with color, then select part of image to add more color to creating focus. (See example 1.)

- Use just lace paper over the image the same way tissue was applied. (See example 2.)

- Try using both lace and tissue in different parts of the work to compare differences. (See example 3.)

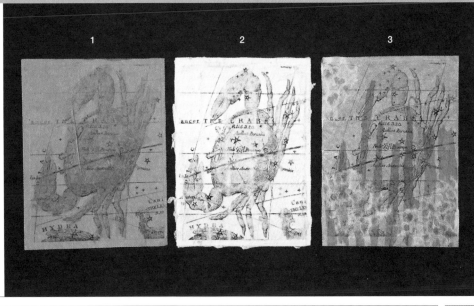

1 2 3

Paper Play

THE EDGES OF THE PAPER have a lot to say about how it will affect the visual impact. Sharp edges are very distinct, concise, and clear. Torn or frayed edges lead the eye softly with little or no definition. It is up to the artist to learn when distinction or softness are best used. These exercises will help you to recognize when to choose a particular effect.

UNIT

8

一位「槍合」聲問就起身分
為台灣的小門選擇是撰為台灣
選擇有現寫，是撰空女正
經過是入一，武」
女正過空，

一入一彩頭色迷，
射擊靶位彩的衣
平頭，都一
壯碩，約見記
布起身。

Artist: Judy Wise

Cutting

- papers of choice to play with
- scissors
- craft knife and cutting surface
- watercolor paper or substrate with background of choice
- imagery, printed or patterned paper
- pencil
- ruler

LEARNING OBJECTIVE: To look at sharp, distinct edges and how they work.

INSTRUCTIONS

STEP 1: Cut out images along their distinct edge using either scissors or craft knife.

STEP 2: Apply imagery to the background.

STEP 3: Continue to "finish" the work in choice of collage techniques.

Note: For this exercise it might serve well to make copies of the same images to play with so notations can be made to how the different applications change the impact and appearance.

FOOD FOR THOUGHT

- If you use copies of the same image to perform this exercise, it will be easier to make comparisons.

- How does containing the entire image within a hard shape differ visually from placing a partial image within the same shape?

- Which is more effective, and why?

- What is appealing and unappealing about cutting along the edge of an image?

Play and Experiment

EXAMPLE 1: Cut out the image and place it in a simple geometric shape.

EXAMPLE 2: Cut out the image and apply to a background and add phrase or quote.

EXAMPLE 3: Repeat above but instead of containing the whole image, place the image off-center in the geometric shape.

EXAMPLE 4: In place of using the edges of the image to cut along, draw a geometric shape around the image to contain it.

Tearing

- Papers and/or images of choice to play with
- scissors
- watercolor paper or substrate with background of choice
- imagery, printed, and/or patterned paper
- pencil
- metal-edged ruler

LEARNING OBJECTIVE: To explore the effects of tearing papers and how it can create greater depth and more cohesion.

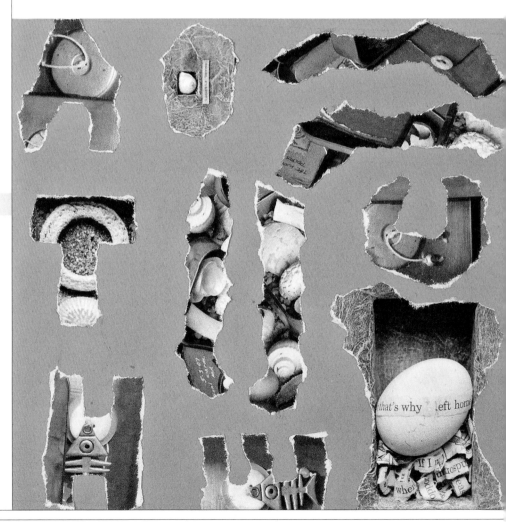

INSTRUCTIONS

STEP 1: Tear out images along their outline either just on the line or just outside the line as desired.

STEP 2: Apply imagery to the background.

STEP 3: Continue to "finish" the work, using your choice of collage techniques.

Play and Experiment

- Tear an image into small squares and form a composition, using the squares to define your image.

- Copy an image. Tear the image out for the collage, then tear the copy into thin strips to write on over, under, or around the image.

- Copy an image. Tear the image out for the collage, then tear the copy or copies into small pieces to use for the background.

Finished collage from torn pieces at left

FOOD FOR THOUGHT

- Tearing images into small squares is a good way to use work that has ended up in the discard pile.

- What do you have on hand you could recycle in this manner?

- How does using the same image in multiple ways in the collage help or hurt its cohesiveness?

Punching

Materials

- craft punches (whatever you have on hand)
- papers of choice to play with
- watercolor paper or substrate with background of choice
- imagery, printed, or patterned paper

LEARNING OBJECTIVE: To use commercially available tools to create forms and shapes to work with.

INSTRUCTIONS

STEP 1: Using punches, create a pile of shapes to play with.

STEP 2: Pile the punched shapes on top of one another to create a collage. It doesn't have to be a large collage; something less than 3" (7.6 cm) square will work.

STEP 3: Repeat, using different punches out of different papers together.

Play and Experiment

- After creating your small samples, paint over them. Let dry and then dry-brush with a light color. Repeat with lighter color, then one more time with metallic paint (left).

- Create a grid collage of the same 5 or 6 punched shapes used different ways (below).

FOOD FOR THOUGHT

- How does painting over the shapes change their impact?

- List ten ways to use punches in collage.

- Make a journal of punched shapes and how you use them.

Burning

- papers of choice to play with
- scissors
- watercolor paper or substrate with background of choice
- pencil
- glue stick or matte medium
- incense and small glass to hold it while not using it
- matches
- small container of water

LEARNING OBJECTIVE: To add an aged look and distinctive edges to paper, using burning.

INSTRUCTIONS

STEP 1: Cut or tear paper samples to work with into small shapes.

STEP 2: Light the incense and burn the edges of your shapes by placing the incense right up against the edge of the paper and moving slowing up or down its length. If it is burning too quickly, simply move the incense away and gently blow on the paper.

STEP 3: Repeat until all edges are burned.

STEP 4: Holes can be burned into central areas by pushing the incense head on against the paper with gentle, steady pressure and blowing lightly.

STEP 5: Make sure to keep the incense in the glass jar when not using it, to avoid a fire hazard, and keep the water container close by should something ignite.

STEP 6: Using glue or matte medium, adhere samples to watercolor paper or substrate of choice.

Note: The temperature at which paper will ignite is 451°F (233°C). The incense burns at a much lower temperature but will still burn the paper; it's more as if it is smoldering the paper. Do not use matches or candles to burn the edges. The paper will reach igniting temperature too quickly and is not easily controlled.

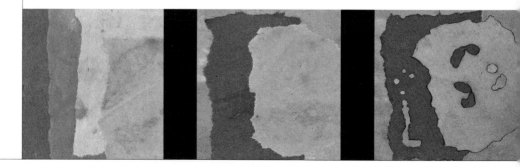

Play and Experiment

- Make copies of imagery and cut and burn one copy; tear and burn the second.

- Make copies of imagery and burn edges but nothing central on one, burn both areas on another, and finally, burn only in the central area but not edges.

- Try to burn an image to appear as though it has been in a fire.

- Pulling different kinds of paper from your stash, try burning them and see how they react. Make notes and keep in a journal for future reference.

Collage of ink-dyed papers torn then burned to shape over tissue background

FOOD FOR THOUGHT

- Does a cut edge or a torn edge burn more easily?

- What kinds of papers burn more quickly than others?

- How difficult was it to burn the paper to make it appear as though it had been in a fire? What worked and what didn't?

Mediums

THERE IS SUCH AN EXCITING ARRAY of mediums available today that it makes it very difficult to choose which one might work for a given project. There are, however, some tried-and-true mediums that have always and will always work well for collage. It doesn't mean there are others available that can't do a better job; it means that only through experience and experimentation will you find what works best for you. Try everything you can and find what suits you.

UNIT 9

SCARLET TANAGER

Artist: LK Ludwig

Gel| Medium

- heavy gel (matte or gloss)
- watercolor paper or background substrate of choice
- imagery
- scissors or craft knife and cutting surface
- dark color of acrylic paint
- water
- flat paintbrush

Note: My preference for mediums is Golden Products, but as stated earlier, there are plenty of manufacturers with good products.

LEARNING OBJECTIVE: To explore one of the many uses of gel medium as a transparent texture.

INSTRUCTIONS

STEP 1: Cut or tear your imagery and papers to apply to background. (See A.)

STEP 2: Use the heavy gel to both adhere and coat papers and imagery.

STEP 3: Let dry.

STEP 4: Add mark making or other imagery to complete collage. (See B.)

STEP 5: Apply a second and/or third coat of heavy gel to the surface to create texture. Let brush marks and skips show. (See C.)

STEP 6: Let dry.

STEP 7: Mix a light wash with dark acrylic paint and coat the surface to expose cracks and crevices. (See D.)

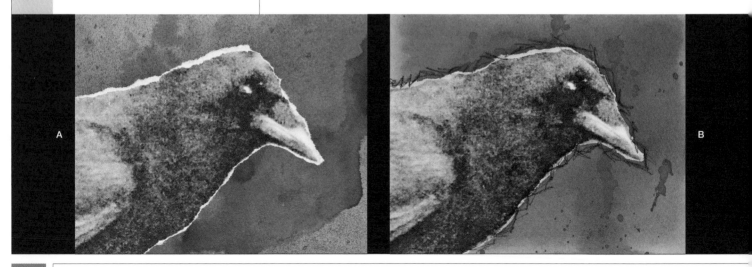

A

B

Play and Experiment

- Try using a sponge to apply the final layer of gel medium for more texture.

- Apply a thick layer of gel medium and use the wrong end of a paintbrush to write in it. Allow to dry overnight and apply a thin dark acrylic paint wash.

- Try a transfer using a black-and-white fresh toner copy. Put down a layer of gel medium on the surface you want to transfer to. Put a layer of gel medium on the toner image. Lay image facedown while still wet over wet surface. Burnish with the bowl of a spoon until smooth and then let dry. When dry, rub warm water gently over the paper until it releases completely and leaves the toner image embedded in the gel medium.

Author's work; branches are an example of gel transfer

FOOD FOR THOUGHT

- How much texture actually becomes obvious?

- What could be done to make it more obvious? Less obvious?

C

D

Matte Medium

- watercolor paper or background substrate of choice
- imagery
- lightweight colored, printed, and patterned papers of choice
- scissors
- craft knife and cutting surface
- flat paintbrush
- Stabilo pencil, china marker, or other mark-making tool
- acrylic paint

LEARNING OBJECTIVE: To explore the use of matte medium as a collage tool.

FOOD FOR THOUGHT

- One of the major advantages of matte medium in collage work is its open time. It dries quickly and, after drying, can be worked on with other mediums. Make a list of ten ways this can be advantageous.

- Compare the results of mixing the matte medium with ink verses a metallic powder.

- Keep a journal of results and try mixing other things with the matte medium as a "carrier," such as the little holes resulting from punching paper for a three-ring binder.

INSTRUCTIONS

STEP 1: Cut or tear your imagery and papers to apply to collage. (See A.)

STEP 2: Use the matte medium to both adhere and coat papers and imagery. Let dry. (See B.)

STEP 3: Using the mark-making tool of choice, add writing or drawing over collage. (See C.)

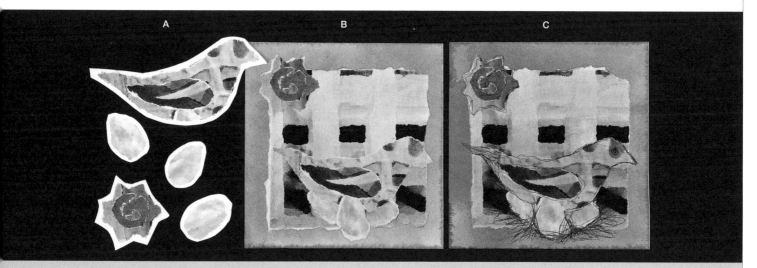

Play and Experiment

EXAMPLE 1: Mix ink with matte medium and use it to add sheer, allover color to the surface of collage.

EXAMPLE 2: Mix metallic products such as Pearl Ex (from Jacquard) with the matte medium to apply a shimmer to portions of the collage.

EXAMPLE 3: Mix ink with matte medium and create a border on the collage.

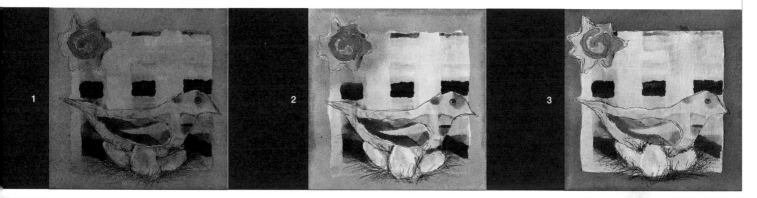

Adhering

- white craft glue
- heavy gel medium
- spackle
- mat board, canvas board, or similar heavy substrate cut into 4" x 5" (10.2 x 12.7 cm) pieces
- small, flat paintbrush
- flat metal washers or metal objects to work with
- ink
- acrylic paint
- gesso

LEARNING OBJECTIVE: To discover options for adhering paper and objects in a collage and how they affect the following layers of collage.

INSTRUCTIONS

STEP 1: Using washers or other metal objects, create eight boards, using the four different types of adhering mediums: household glue (A), spackle (B), tacky craft glue (C), and lastly, heavy gel medium (D).

STEP 2: Mark the backs of your boards with pencil, noting which adhering medium you used.

STEP 3: Allow all boards to dry overnight.

STEP 4: Take four of the eight boards (one of each set of two) and coat with gesso. Allow to dry.

A

B

C

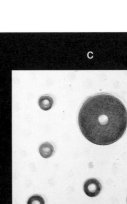

D

Play and Experiment

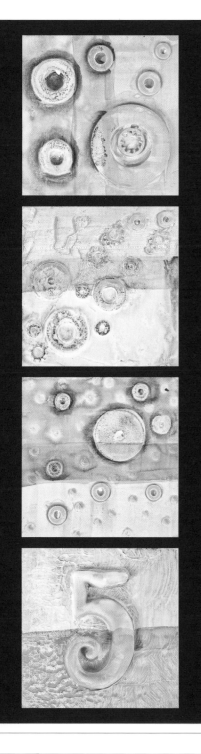

- Coat one side of each board (with and without gesso) with and ink wash. (See left.)
- Coat the other side of each board (with and without gesso) with a paint wash. (See below.)
- Make more boards and play with straight paint, ink, or glazes.

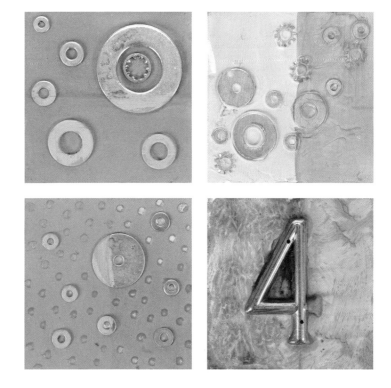

FOOD FOR THOUGHT

- Of the four adhesives used, which had no visible effect on the subsequent layers?
- Which held faster and stronger?
- Which adhesives act as a resist?
- What do they resist?

Paints

- watercolor paper or background substrate of choice in small pieces approximately 4" x 5" (10.2 x 12.7 cm)
- imagery
- lightweight colored, printed, and patterned papers of choice
- chip brush
- matte medium
- acrylic paint (one light, one medium, and one dark color that work well together)
- small sponge

LEARNING OBJECTIVE: To explore of a few of the many uses of paint in a collage.

INSTRUCTIONS

STEP 1: Using the imagery and paper, create small 4" x 5" (10.2 x 12.7 cm) quick collages by cutting or tearing the pieces. You don't need to cover the entire background for this exercise.

STEP 2: Use matte medium to adhere the pieces to the substrate, then coat lightly. Let dry.

STEP 3: Starting with the darkest color of acrylic paint, lightly brush paint over areas of the collage, diffusing some of the imagery and paper, leaving other areas alone and filling in parts but not all of the background. (See A.)

STEP 4: Repeat with a medium color. (See B.)

STEP 5: Repeat finally with the lightest color. (See C.)

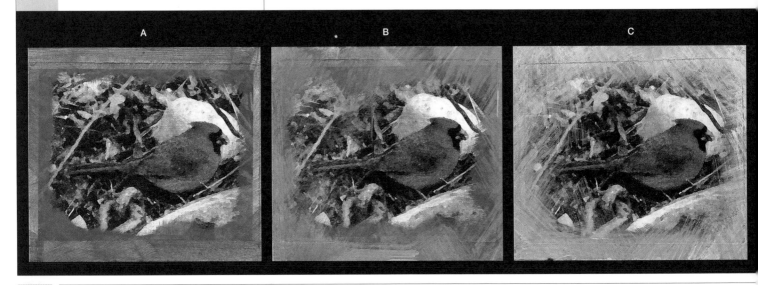

Play and Experiment

EXAMPLE 1: Use a wash of paint on all or most of the imagery.

EXAMPLE 2: Try sponging the paint on in places rather than brushing.

EXAMPLE 3: Use a wash of ink mixed with matte medium on all or part of the imagery.

1

2

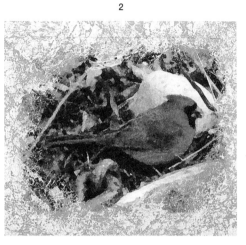

3

FOOD FOR THOUGHT

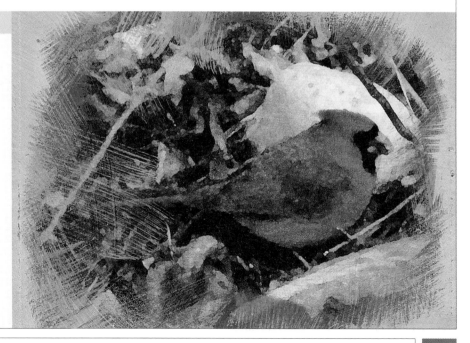

- How does a light wash change the look of a piece versus a dark wash?

- How does a monochromatic paint approach differ in appearance from a compatible color approach?

- Paint is really one of the most versatile tools available for collage—it's right up there with paper. List ten ways you could use paint that you didn't try in this exercise.

Inks

- watercolor paper or background substrate of choice
- imagery
- lightweight colored, printed, and patterned papers of choice
- scissors or craft knife and cutting surface
- flat paintbrush
- small, round detail paintbrush (or several sizes if readily available)
- permanent black (or other color) pen (personal favorite is the fine-tipped Uni-Ball)
- pencil
- inks in bottle

LEARNING OBJECTIVE: To discover ways to use ink as if it were paint.

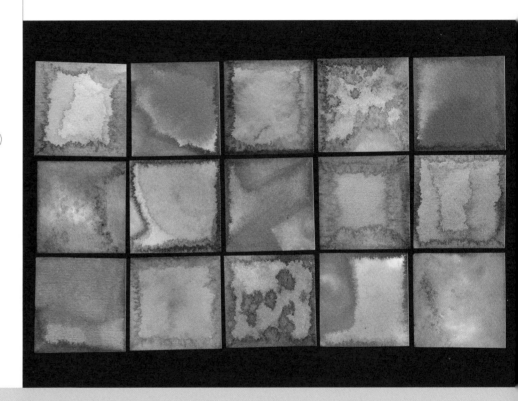

FOOD FOR THOUGHT

- What happens to the ink when it crosses over other ink that is already dry?
- How does sanding affect the way the paper pulls in the ink?

- Does a washed ink background accept new ink differently?
- List five other ways to use ink in collage.

INSTRUCTIONS

STEP 1: Using the imagery and paper, create small 4" x 5" (10.2 x 12.7 cm) quick collages by cutting or tearing the pieces. (It's not necessary to cover the entire background for this exercise.)

STEP 2: Use matte medium to adhere the pieces to the substrate, then coat them lightly with ink. Let dry.

STEP 3: Using pencil lightly sketch or write on and around the piece. Accent the imagery, write over parts of it, doodle, whatever comes naturally. Keep in mind this is just an exercise and not a final masterpiece. Just let things happen freely.

Play and Experiment

- Try washing larger areas with diluted ink before going in with detail brush and adding more.

- Treat the ink as if it was watercolor.

- Using the ink as if it was paint, fill in areas of the work as the eye suggests. (See example for hints.)

- Using the permanent black pen, go over your sketching and/or writing as desired to give more detail. Add more if it feels right.

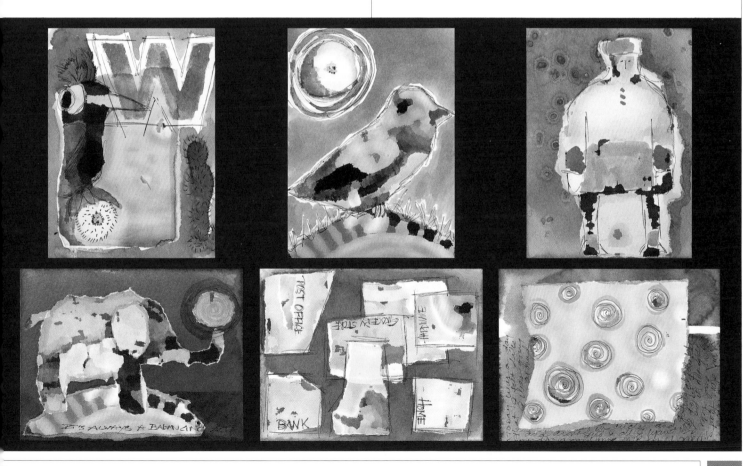

Imagery

THE OLD SAYING GOES that a picture paints a thousand words, and it couldn't be truer. Images relate not just whole sentences but paragraphs in a minimum of space. The impact of an image is affected by many factors: how it relates to the rest of the piece, how much importance it is given or not. Being subtle is sometimes the most direct way of delivering a message or thought. Playing with images will open new horizons and lead to paths yet unknown.

Artist: Stephanie Lee

Photos

- photographs of various types: vintage or copies of them, emulsion photos, digital professionally printed photos or ink-jet photos (Photos should have no personal meaning for this exercise, to allow for more freedom in experimentation.)
- water
- oil pastels (inexpensive brands work fine for this)
- pan pastels if available
- large needle or scratching tool
- water

LEARNING OBJECTIVE: To explore the effects of techniques on different types of photographs.

INSTRUCTIONS

STEP 1: Select several photos to work with. Black-and-white works best. (See A.)

STEP 2: Wet photo and pat damp dry.

STEP 3: Lightly sand the surface in varying degrees. Lightly rub oil pastel into photo. (See B.)

STEP 4: Using scratching tool or large needle, doodle shapes, words, or outline imagery on the photo surface. Rub dark color oil pastel such as black or brown into deep scratches, then wipe off surface. Apply second and third colors to complete. (See C.)

STEP 5: Working in layers, apply the oil pastel building up to bright and vibrant color. (See D.)

Play and Experiment

- Repeat with all kinds of photos in the stash to see how they react. Take note of which type is being worked on before it's worked.

- Using inexpensive glossy photo paper, an ink-jet printer, and watercolor paper, try a water transfer as follows: Print out image on glossy photo paper. Wet the surface of the watercolor paper with warm water. Lay the color print on the glossy wet watercolor paper, ink side down, and burnish with a paper towel. Be careful not to let photo slide. Burnish with the back of a spoon and peel back photo to reveal transfer. (Example 1 is photo after transfer. Example 2 is actual transfer.)

Above: Photo paper after transfer
Below: Water transfer

1

2

FOOD FOR THOUGHT

- Make note of the results obtained over various types of photos and keep for reference.

- Which was most effective?

- Which was least effective?

- List five ways you could alter the surface of the photo and what tool you would use.

Drawings

- drawing pencils of varying types
- good art eraser
- easy-rolling black pen
- white sketch paper or copy paper

LEARNING OBJECTIVE: To begin to practice drawing using simple mark making.

INSTRUCTIONS

STEP 1: Using the various pencils on paper, draw the following: circles, loops, light lines, dark lines, spirals, squares, basically anything you think of. The idea is to learn how the drawing instrument you choose will respond.

STEP 2: Repeat above exercise with a pen.

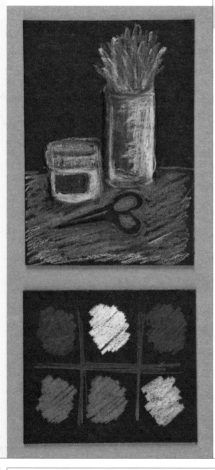

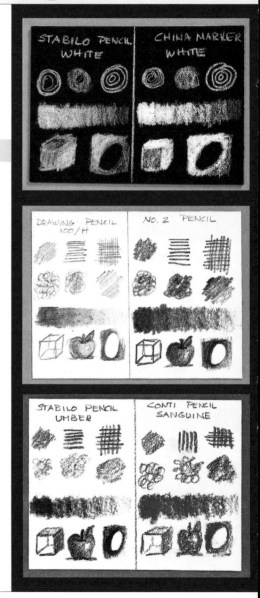

Play and Experiment

- Run an eraser through the pencil mark-making exercise to observe which types of pencils erase more easily than do others.

- Expand the types of marks made and try drawing actual objects such as a piece of fruit or stack of books.

- Try contour drawing, which is simply drawing the outline of something; the line defines the edges of what is being drawn.

- Try cross-contour drawing. This is where the lines hint at the direction of the form. It doesn't have to be exact; in fact, the opposite applies here. More energy will be evident if expressive lines are used versus grid-type lines.

- Try adding shadowing to your forms, using the sides of the pencil or by crosshatching with the pen.

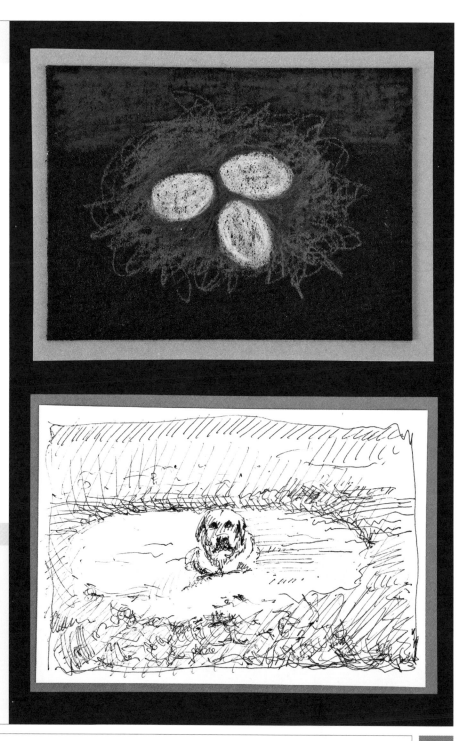

Mud Puppy Sketch (cross-contour drawing) by Lowell Shay

FOOD FOR THOUGHT

- Which type of pencils did you like best? Why?

- List/describe the preferences for sketching on sketch paper.

- List/describe the preferences for sketching on newsprint.

- List five ways to create shadows.

Brayer Play

- soft brayer(s) of various widths (2", 4", and/or 6" [5.1, 10.2, and/or 15.2 cm])
- water-soluble printing ink or acrylic paints
- waxed paper or palette
- pad of newsprint
- flat things to print (leaves, feathers, herbs, ferns, lace, keys, cutouts, etc.)

LEARNING OBJECTIVE: To become familiar and comfortable with the many uses of a brayer in laying down a printed background and overprinting imagery.

INSTRUCTIONS

STEP 1: Tape waxed paper (about 18" [45.7 cm] in length) to work surface or use a palette.

STEP 2: Squeeze a small amount of ink or paint onto one side of your waxed paper.

STEP 3: Roll brayer through ink repeatedly to coat the brayer surface evenly. The ink or paint will "tack up" and feel a bit sticky when ready to print.

STEP 4: Place your printable piece on your newsprint.

STEP 5: Roll inked brayer over piece *once*.

STEP 6: Lift piece to reveal print.

Play and Experiment

- Print using two colors. Load color onto printing matter with one brayer, lay printable piece on paper and roll over with a brayer loaded with a different color.

- Lay printable piece under paper and roll brayer over top.

- Load ink or paint onto printable piece on palette, transfer printable piece to paper, and lay a second piece of paper on top, rubbing with your fingers.

- Print with flat, nonorganic matter such as keys or coins.

- Mix colors on the palette before loading the brayer.

- Mix colors on the palette but do not mix completely.

- Try printing on different types of paper.

FOOD FOR THOUGHT

- Which of the chosen printing items worked best? Why?

- List at least five other things to try printing with.

- Is there a personal preference for ink or paint or would it depend on the particular piece?

- Which dries faster, paint or ink?

- Which papers were tried and what were the results?

Borrowed

- copies of images or personal work (copy images in different sizes to work with)
- watercolor paper or background substrate of choice
- flat paintbrush
- matte medium
- gesso and/or acrylic paint
- pencil
- scissors and/or craft knife and cutting surface

LEARNING OBJECTIVE: To explore borrowing imagery in a composition.

INSTRUCTIONS

STEP 1: Choose one image to work with. Tear or cut the largest copy of the image to use as a background.

STEP 2: Using matte medium, collage image to substrate.

STEP 3: Take an enlarged version of image to be borrowed and cut or tear out.

STEP 4: Using matte medium, place the image in the foreground.

STEP 5: Complete the collage with your choice of techniques.

Robin always loved the color red.

Play and Experiment

- Try using larger portions of the image over a smaller version in the background.
- Create a grid-style background with image torn or cut into squares, then collage a larger image on top. Add even larger details as the final step.

- List five more ways you can borrow an image and use it in the same collage.
- How does it differ in effect when small is layered over large versus large over small?

Drawing Over

- black-and-white laser copies that have been lightened significantly
- black permanent pen (such as Uni-Ball)
- drawing pencil
- art eraser
- gesso
- flat paintbrush

LEARNING OBJECTIVE: To discover ways to create the illusion of drawing.

INSTRUCTIONS

STEP 1: Start with a photo and make a light black-and-white copy. (See A and B.)

STEP 2: Lay down a very thin wash of gesso over all of your copy and let dry. (See C.)

STEP 3: Start with the pencil and go over the prominent outlines of the subject of the photo. Use a sketching motion, not a detail motion. Just try and capture the gist of the image. (See D.)

STEP 4: Go over the piece one more time and add shadows and details. (See E.)

A   B   C   D   E

Play and Experiment

- Try using just the black pen. Make the drawing very sketchy in appearance.

- Go for extreme detail in your drawing and take your time.

- Try using the same image and approach it different ways (for example, just pencil, just pen, both, lighter and heavier washes of gesso).

FOOD FOR THOUGHT

- Take note of the comfort level as the work progressed. Did the strokes become more daring and less controlled or the opposite?

- Think of ways to incorporate this sketching into a collage.

Visual Dictionary

QUOTES, POETRY, PHRASES, and even single words all have a place in a collage. The use of the written word is not necessary but can often enhance a collage piece in a way no image, color, or texture can. The words can be in the background, the foreground, or even used as a focal point.

Gather up collections of words, quotes, and personal writings, and let's begin to explore the world of the visual dictionary.

UNIT 11

Artist: Michelle Ward

From the Heart

- copies of imagery that has strong personal meaning
- pen (Uni-Ball or fine-line Sharpie recommended)
- pencil
- writing paper
- tissue paper
- watercolor paper or background substrate
- matte medium

LEARNING OBJECTIVE: To open up the channels of communication between the heart and the hand.

INSTRUCTIONS

STEP 1: Adhere the imagery to substrates, using matte medium. Create a single image or a composition, whichever feels most comfortable. Don't spend a lot of time; work quickly.

STEP 2: Think about the image while you are working. Let dry. (See A.)

STEP 3: While the images are drying, sit with each one in turn and write the thoughts that come to mind. Write quickly and do not wordsmith. Work intuitively. (See B.)

STEP 4: When each piece is dry, sit with the image and the words and circle the words or phrases that feel most important and best express what you are trying to communicate. (See C.)

STEP 5: One piece at a time, look at the words and the image together and choose which word or words to add to the piece and where to place them.

A

B

C

Play and Experiment

EXAMPLE 1: Write directly on the piece with pen and/or pencil. Stabilo pencils work very well for this and come in white, black, and brown.

EXAMPLE 2: Using tissue paper and pen, write the words, let dry (heating it for a second or two with the hair dryer helps as well), then use the matte medium to adhere the tissue to the work. Laying a layer of matte medium down first, then applying when wet, will make the tissue "melt" or disappear for the most part, leaving just the words visible.

EXAMPLE 3: Type the words or phrases on your computer and print them out. Tear or cut out and add.

FOOD FOR THOUGHT

- How does having the image in visual range help or not help when writing?

- Did what you originally thought about the image and what you ended up using surprise you? In what way were you surprised?

- When doing a comparison of the same image with different word approaches, which were more effective in the communication, and why?

- Did you develop a preference for working with words?

LAB 46 — Drawing on Experience

Materials

- notebook or sketchbook
- pencil and/or pen
- camera
- matte medium
- small, flat paintbrush
- watercolor paper or journal

INSTRUCTIONS

STEP 1: By getting out of our ordinary experience, we find ways to change perspective on everyday observances. Hop on a bus or a train or go to the mall and get out the sketchbook and camera, then start observing.

STEP 2: Collages are everywhere, mostly in the form of advertisements.

STEP 3: Make sketches, take notes, and/or take photographs of anything that pulls your eye. Drink it all in and bring it back to your work space.

STEP 4: Print out pictures and lay them out on table. (See right.)

STEP 5: Put your notes together with the photos.

STEP 6: Choose the two that stand out most and work with them in the next section.

LEARNING OBJECTIVE: To find ways to look for inspiration in the everyday surroundings. (This exercise is best done as a "field trip" but can be done at home.)

Play and Experiment

- Design and execute a collage that reflects your personal observations. (See example 1.)

- Design and execute a collage that imitates that shape but not the content. (See example 2.)

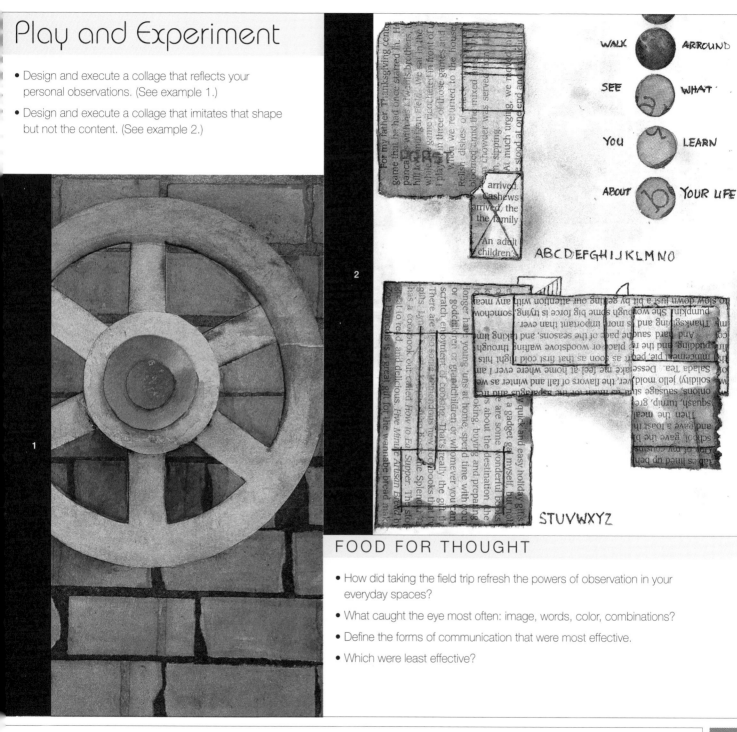

1

2

WALK ARROUND

SEE WHAT

YOU LEARN

ABOUT YOUR LIFE

ABCDEFGHIJKLMNO

STUVWXYZ

FOOD FOR THOUGHT

- How did taking the field trip refresh the powers of observation in your everyday spaces?

- What caught the eye most often: image, words, color, combinations?

- Define the forms of communication that were most effective.

- Which were least effective?

Borrowed Words

Materials

- collection of quotes to work with printed onto paper that can be cut or torn
- watercolor paper or background substrate of choice
- small, flat paintbrush
- matte medium
- imagery that works well with chosen quotes
- small bits of scrap paper

LEARNING OBJECTIVE: To explore the use of quotes in a composition. When using quotes, you must always provide attribution. For this exercise, I give my humblest thanks to Kahlil Gibran for his beautiful words on generosity.

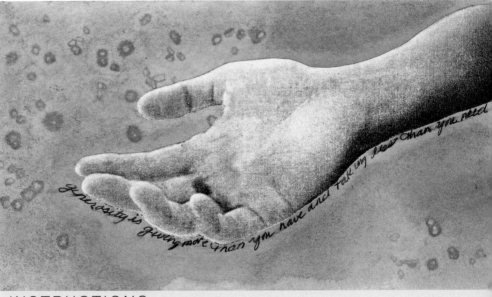

INSTRUCTIONS

STEP 1: Choose a quote and imagery to work with.

STEP 2: Adhere the imagery to the background substrate with matte medium. Let dry.

STEP 3: Work quote into the composition either in whole or part.

Play and Experiment

- Try using part of the quote in an overscaled copy as a background. Diffuse with a wash of gesso or paint. Then add imagery and quote. (See right top.)

- Using the imagery as the background, repeat the quote in whole or part all over or in various parts of the collage.

- Try making a basic textured background. Enlarge the print of the quote so that the enclosed areas of the letters (for example, the circle that is formed in a capital O) are large enough to add imagery to. (See below right.)

FOOD FOR THOUGHT

- Does the content of the quote have a lot or little effect on how you choose to communicate it?

- Which is more effective, making the words or the image predominant?

- Does repeating the words carry the communication more strongly, or is it overbearing?

- Which was the most satisfying piece you completed, and why?

Vintage Documents

- stash of ephemera (vintage letters, bills, postcards, statements, etc.)
- small, flat paintbrush
- matte medium
- watercolor paper or background substrate of choice
- imagery
- scraps of decorative papers
- acrylic paint

LEARNING OBJECTIVE: To look for meaning and connections in vintage imagery to use in a collage composition.

INSTRUCTIONS

STEP 1: Choose an image with words to start with, such as an old advertisement, and decide what communication to articulate. (See A.)

STEP 2: Use gesso to diffuse and obscure parts of the ephemera that have no bearing on the piece, and highlight those that do. Let dry. (See B.)

STEP 3: Begin to add the imagery, connecting the words that have been left showing with the images on or around them. (See C.)

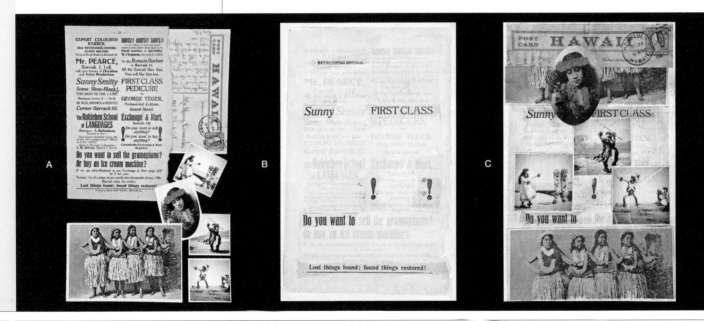

Play and Experiment

- Make copies of chosen image and ephemera and make several versions of the collage for comparison.

- Try altering copies of the same image five different ways.

- Change the scale of your original. Try working with it larger and smaller.

- Turn your image into a transparency and try overlaying it with other images.

FOOD FOR THOUGHT

- Which is more effective: the written word or the image? Why?

- How does changing the scale of an image or word(s) change its communication?

- What was the impetus for making the choice of words to accompany the imagery?

- Did you effectively communicate what you started out to or did the message change as the piece progressed?

Unification and Composition

A SUCCESSFUL COLLAGE is not just some pretty images and words thrown down without intent or planning. It might look good but, like all shallow beauty, interest will fade quickly if there is no depth. Success is achieved by unifying the elements of the collage, connecting them with meaning or content, and creating a good composition. Here we will take a short walk through a few final steps to a successful piece that communicates its content and is pleasing to the viewer.

UNIT

12

Artist: Judi Riesch

Palette

- copies of personal collages or other people's collages from books or magazines
- pen or pencil
- watercolor paper or journal
- glue stick
- small box of watercolors (inexpensive is fine) or colored pencils

LEARNING OBJECTIVE: To explore the power of color and how to use it.

Play and Experiment

- Using a hot palette, tear or cut shapes to form a collage.
- Repeat, using the same shapes but changing the palette to a cool palette.
- Repeat, this time using black and white.
- Repeat one more time, using a monochromatic palette.

FOOD FOR THOUGHT

- Pull out the original work and compare with your experiments.
- How does the message change with color?
- What colors would you try if you did it again, and why?
- Which palette tells this particular story best? Why?

INSTRUCTIONS

STEP 1: Choose one collage to work with at a time. Make black and white photocopies. (See A.)

STEP 2: With the original hidden, take a photocopy and using watercolors or colored pencils, add color using a monochromatic palette. (See B.)

STEP 3: Use just brown (or sepia), black, and white. (See C.)

STEP 4: With watercolors or colored pencils, add color using a water (cool) palette (blues, greens, plums). (See D.)

STEP 5: Repeat, using complementary colors of choice. (See E.)

STEP 6: Repeat, using a hot palette—yellows, reds, oranges. (See F.)

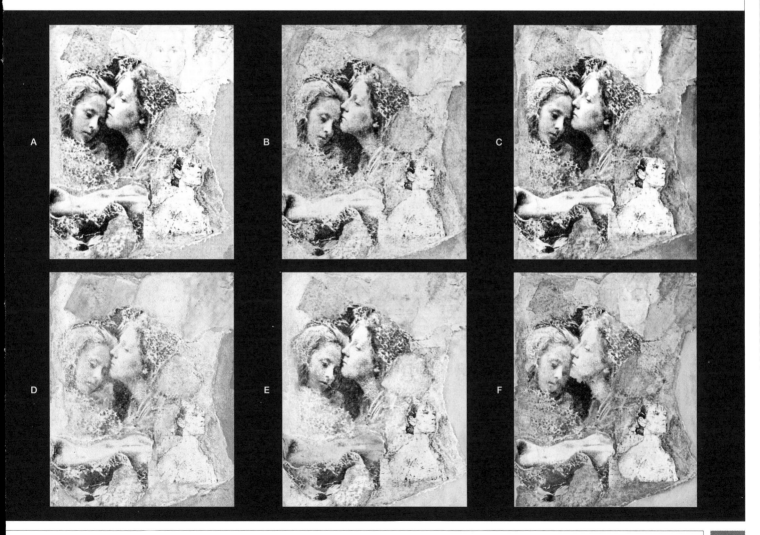

Content

- list of words you like (e.g., bird, fish, eyes, spirit, create)
- watercolor paper or background substrate of your choice
- small, flat paintbrush
- matte medium
- images that relate to your chosen words
- printouts of the words in different fonts and sizes
- acrylic paints
- scraps of decorative paper

LEARNING OBJECTIVE: To investigate ways to communicate a message.

INSTRUCTIONS

STEP 1: Choose a word and related images.

STEP 2: Work quickly. You are only communicating one word at a time, and this is an exercise not a masterpiece.

STEP 3: With paint or paper or a combination, create a simple background.

STEP 4: Adhere image(s) with matte medium to background.

STEP 5: Choose the font and size of the word that best fits your composition.

Play and Experiment

- Reverse images and words. Place the word down first from an overscaled copy and lay image(s) over it.

- Stop when images are down and let dry briefly. Make copies. Try variations of the word applications to compare with one another.

"Booby egg:" Michelle Unger. All other photos and images: Bee Shay.

FOOD FOR THOUGHT

- Choose a piece and make a list of thoughts that come to mind when you look at it. Ask someone else to do the same without discussion. Compare the visual impact and perceptions.

- Which pieces communicate their intent most clearly? Why?

Good, Bad, and Just Not Right

- two L-shaped pieces of black or white cardstock (viewfinder)
- six color copies of an image that has many elements or details (see example)
- note paper or journal
- pen or pencil
- glue stick
- scissors or craft knife and cutting surface

LEARNING OBJECTIVE: To discover what makes a composition communicate exactly what you are trying to say.

INSTRUCTIONS

STEP 1: Choose one image and make all six copies.

STEP 2: Using the viewfinder over the first copy, find the first most interesting and pleasing portions of the image.

STEP 3: Run a pencil or pen line to mark it off.

STEP 4: Remove the viewfinder, cut along lines, and set aside.

STEP 5: Repeat five more times.

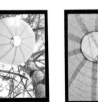

Play and Experiment

- Once you have all six of your compositions, line them up and make notes on what each one says and how it says it.

- Use a piece of your own work that you were unhappy with.

- Use a piece of your own work that you were happy with.

FOOD FOR THOUGHT

- Does reducing the elements of an image make a clearer communication?

- Is busy better or is it too much information?

- Does color affect how the piece communicates with regard to composition?

- Turn a successful piece upside down and squint. Does it still feel balanced and pleasing to the eye? What does that tell you?

finishes

- commercially prepared glaze or transparent acrylic paint in dark colors (such as Golden's fluid acrylic paint)
- ink
- matte medium or any common clear sealer, matte or gloss finish
- substrate with finished collage

LEARNING OBJECTIVE: To understand ways to unify the surface either in process or upon completion.

INSTRUCTIONS

STEP 1: Prepare a 12" x 12" (30.5 x 30.5 cm) collage by applying a thin sealer coat. Let dry. Repeat.

STEP 2: Cut collage into smaller pieces and try different glazes and finishes for comparison.

STEP 3: Apply a thin layer of glaze as suggested in Play and Experiment. If you apply too much, remove quickly with dry cloth. For stubborn areas, a damp cloth may work. Do not wet the substrate completely.

STEP 4: Add another layer of glaze if sufficient coverage was not met.

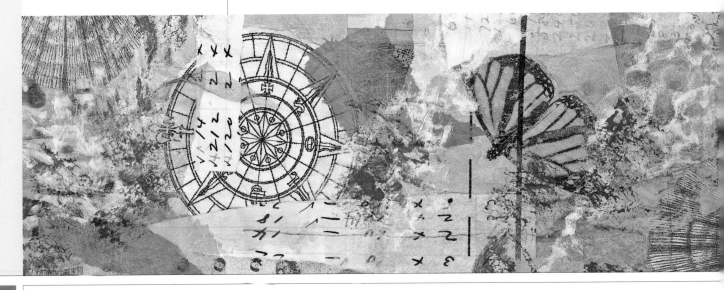

Play and Experiment

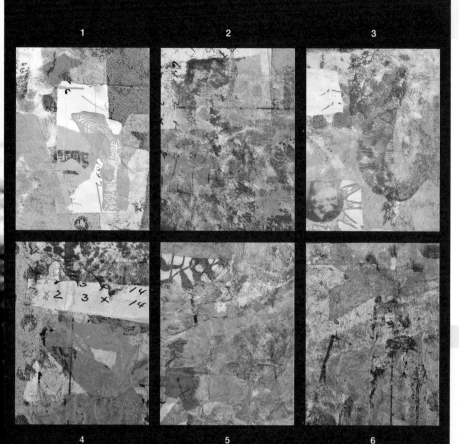

EXAMPLE 1: Keep one piece without glaze for comparison.

EXAMPLE 2: Mix ink with matte medium for a glaze.

EXAMPLE 3: Use a wash of acrylic paint for a glaze.

EXAMPLE 4: Try straight ink as a glaze.

EXAMPLE 5: Mix tube watercolor paint with matte medium for a glaze.

EXAMPLE 6: Use an antiquing solution such as Golden's Asphaltum to add age or definition to texture.

FOOD FOR THOUGHT

- How do different glazes change the same piece?

- Does glazing with a color from your collage unify the piece more effectively than using a white or brown glaze? What are the differences?

Gallery

Give up to grace.

The ocean takes care of each wave till it gets to shore.

Ocean

Ocean

OFFERINGS FROM THE OCEAN

All you need
is deep
within you
waiting to unfold
and
reveal itself.
All you have to do
is be still
and
take time
to seek
what is within,
and you will surely find it.

soul wisdom

Artist: Catherine Anderson

Artist: Tracie Bunkers

Artist: Sue Haddon

Artist: Melissa Manley

last night as

SLEEPING, I DREAMT - MARVELLOUS ERROR! - THAT A
OUT IN MY HEART I SAID: ALONG WHICH SECRET AQUEDUCT
COMING TO ME, WATER OF NEW LIFE THAT I HAVE NEVER
LAST NIGHT, AS I WAS SLEEPING - I DREAMT - DRUNK.
MARVELLOUS ERROR! - THAT I HAD A BEEHIVE,
HERE IN MY HEART. AND THE GOLDEN BEES WERE
MAKING WHITE COMBS AND SWEET HONEY FROM MY
OLD FAILURES. LASTNIGHT AS I WAS SLEEPING, I
DREAMT - MARVELLOUS ERROR! - THAT A FIERY
SUN WAS GIVING LIGHT INSIDE MY HEART. IT
WAS FIERY BECAUSE I FELT WARMTH AS FROM
A HEARTH, ANDSUN BECAUSE IT GAVE LIGHT
AND BROUGHT TEARS TO MY EYES.
AS I SLEPT, I DREAMT - MARVELLOUS
ERROR! - THAT IT WAS GOD I HAD
HERE IN MY HEART.

Artist: Gina Armfield

Artist: Jan Harris

...hoes of past heard in blessings

a life lived

SEASIDE INCOME
PROPERTY

Contributors and Resources

CONTRIBUTORS

Cathy Anderson
cathy@catherineandersonstduio.com
www.catherineandersonstudio.com

Gina Armfield
armfield@att.net
www.sweetsistergina.typepad.com

Anne Bagby
annebagby@bellsouth.net
www.annebagby.com

Traci Bunkers
traci@tracibunkers.com
www.bonkersfiber.com

Shirley Ende-Saxe
rgrace44223@yahoo.com
www.shirleyendesaxe.typepad.com

Jen Goff
paperwingsdiy@gmail.com
www.paperwingspdx.com

Sue Hadden
soozihadden@yahoo.com

Jan Harris
purplebirdart@q.com
www.purplebirdart.blogspot.com

Katie Kendrick
joyouslybecoming@earthlink.net
www.joyouslybecoming.typepad.com

Laura Kinney
Lauraakinney@msn.com

Stephanie Lee
stephanielee@q.com
www.stephanielee.typepad.com

LK Ludwig
ludwiglk@gmail.com
www.gryphonsfeather.typepad.com

Melissa Manley
melissamanleymetal@yahoo.com
www.melissamanleystudios.com

Misty Mawn
mistymawn@gmail.com
www.mistymawn.typepad.com

Laurie Mika
laurie@mikaarts.com
www.mikaarts.com

Fred Mullett
fredb@fredbmullett.com
www.fredbmullett.com

Lynne Perrella
lkperrella@aol.com
www.lkperrella.com

Judi Riesch
jjriesch@aol.com
www.itsmysite.com/judiriesch/

Michelle Ward
grnpep@optonline.net
www.greenpepperpress.com

Judy Wise
judywise@canby.com
www.judywise.blogspot.com

RESOURCES

Earth Guild
papermaking kits and beautiful
handmade papers
www.earthguild.com

Golden Artist Colors
mediums and paints
www.goldenpaints.com

Green Pepper Press
rubber stamps
www.greenpepperpress.com

Jacquard Products
paint
www.jacquardproducts.com

K & Company
scrapbooking papers
www.kandcompany.com

KI Memories, Inc.
patterned and cut cardstock
www.kimemories.com

Merion Art & Repro Center
fine arts supplies
www.merionart.com

Parchment
fine papers
www.parchmentnantucket.com

Ranger
re-inkers and ink pads
www.rangerink.com

Staedtler
Mastercarve carving block and tools
www.staedtler-usa.com

About the Author

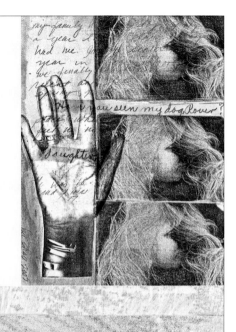

BEE SHAY has been an instructor in the creative arts since 1978 in some way, shape, or form. She identifies herself primarily as a teacher, and is also a nurturer, artist, parent, and friend. In 1994, after painting traditionally for almost twenty-five years, she fell into the world of mixed-media arts and was instantly in love with collage. The subsequent years have been a journey filled with exploration, teaching courses locally and at art retreats nationally, involvement with online art communities, and continually expanding her body of work. The most enjoyable piece of all of this has been "playing the muse" by lighting the flame in her students and watching as they burn brightly, second only to the extended family that has resulted from all this kindred contact.

Author's self portrait

Acknowledgments

I'VE ALWAYS WANTED to write and illustrate a book but somehow in my world, it was going to be a children's book . . . one of the many stories I used to tell my kids over and over again. Perhaps some day the Moonchangers will come to life outside their wee bedrooms, but for now my dream is a reality and I couldn't be more fortunate.

So many people come to mind and as is often is the case at a time like this, I find myself with too little room and too little time to acknowledge them all. You know who you are. I wouldn't be here without your loving support and encouragement to follow my dreams. So my love and heartfelt thanks goes out to you from these pages.

To my readers, thank you for buying this book and taking the journey with me. It is one well worth taking and I hope you reach higher and farther than the edges of the pages. Please feel free to keep me apprised of your progress or shout for help should you get lost.

To Mary Ann, my amazing editor, for putting her faith in me to take on this project and hearing my voice. For keeping me calm and not making me feel like I didn't know what I was doing.

To everyone at Quarry who made this book happen. It was a team effort and without them and their amazing talents this book wouldn't be on the shelves.

To Lynne and LK, thank you for encouraging me to take the leap and more important, for opening the door.

To LK, Judi, Frank, Annette, and Shelley. Thank you for being there for me through this year in a way that only true friends can be by making me laugh, making me cry, and showing me true north when the horizons were lost.

To my fairy godmothers Sooze and Jodes. Where would I be without your fairy dust?

To "the boyz," thanks for keeping my heart and my feet warm during the hard parts.

To Lowie. Thank you for being as patient as you could be and as loving and supportive as you are in my quest for my dream. Thank you for introducing me to the island we now call home in all its beauty and wild abundance of inspiration. For building me a beautiful nest in the trees of our home from which to work. You are a genius and an artist and my biggest hope is that someday you will see that for yourself.

And finally, to my kids, La, Bean and Bud . . . my best work ever. You make me proud every day. How lucky can one person be? I love you all and leave you with a most grateful heart.